Love
Mary

ABOARD AN
AMERICAN
CLASSIC

Steve —

*Hope you never have to sail
an old schooner across the Atlantic —
much better to take the Queen Mary.*

George

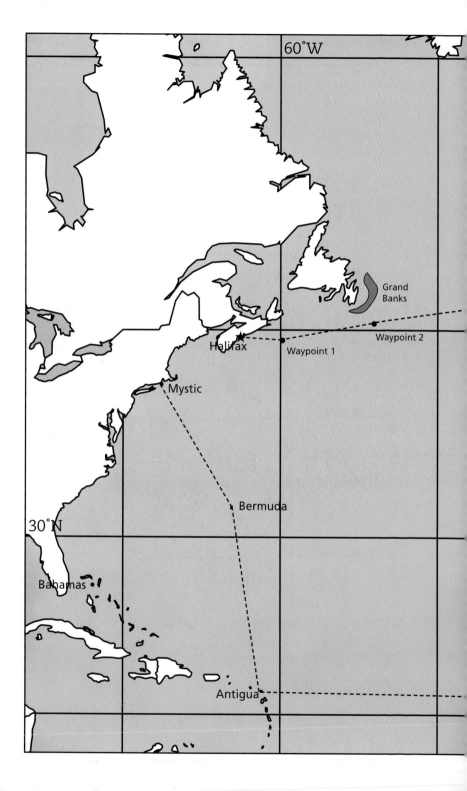

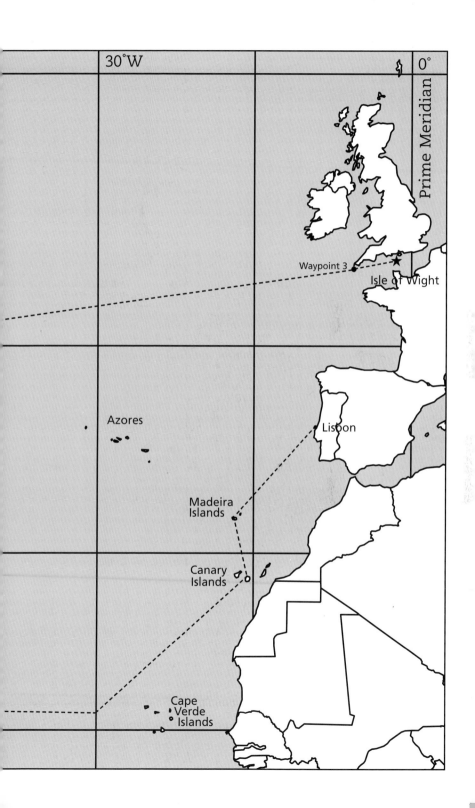

30°W

0°

Prime Meridian

Waypoint 3

Isle of Wight

Azores

Lisbon

Madeira
Islands

Canary
Islands

Cape
Verde
Islands

ABOARD AN AMERICAN CLASSIC

Across the Atlantic with BRILLIANT

GEORGE MOFFETT

Mystic Seaport
Mystic, Connecticut
©2002

Mystic Seaport — The Museum of America and the Sea — is the nation's leading museum presenting the American experience from a maritime perspective. Located along the banks of the historic Mystic River in Mystic, Connecticut, the Museum houses extensive collections representing the material culture of maritime America, and offers educational programs from pre-school to post-graduate.

For more information, call us at 888-9SEAPORT, or visit us on the Web at www.mysticseaport.org

©2002 by Mystic Seaport Museum, Inc.
All rights reserved
First Edition

Cataloging-in-Publication Data

Moffett, George H.
    Aboard an American classic : across the Atlantic with Brilliant /
George Moffett. — 1st ed. — Mystic, Conn. : Mystic Seaport, c2002.
    p. : ill. (chiefly col.), maps ; cm.
    Includes glossary.

    1. Brilliant (Schooner) 2. Tall Ships race, 2000. 3. Yacht racing. I. Title.

GV 832 M6.4 2002
ISBN 0-939510-78-2

Editor: Laura Souhrada Kyle
Design: Linda Cusano

Contents

Appendices

Foreword

Brilliant. The name could not be more appropriate. In the early 1930s an experienced yachtsman wanted a new boat that would meet the highest standards of safety, speed, and beauty. The challenge of designing the boat went to a truly brilliant young designer, Olin Stephens, who was just beginning a brilliant career that would continue into the 21st century. Olin's response to the challenge was remarkable: the boat that he conceived, and which was masterfully built by the Henry B. Nevins yard, brilliantly met all the requirements of her demanding owner and has become one of the most respected classic yachts in existence today.

After 20 eventful years engaged in yachting and in military service, her then owner, Briggs Cunningham, donated *Brilliant* to Mystic Seaport. There, she would serve as the mainstay of the Museum's at-sea sail-education program. This program has been a brilliant success over five decades due to several key factors: *Brilliant* herself; the care she has received over the last 50 years; and most importantly, the dedicated captains she has had. First, Captain Adrian Lane brought his lifetime of sea experience to the task and initiated many of the elements that would give the program its structure. Adrian was followed by Captain Francis "Biff" Bowker, whose experience in coasting schooners during the end of their era gave him a degree of authority that was matched by his good sea-

Foreword

manship and his broad maritime knowledge.

When Biff retired, the Museum was fortunate to have the ideal new skipper literally on board. *Brilliant's* mate for a number of years, George H. Moffett, Jr., was a dedicated sailor and educator. There was no question that George was the one to take the helm; that decision has been proved correct time and time again. George has brought new dimensions to the program, demanded a high level of performance from *Brilliant,* and inspired his crews, young and old, to work toward that same high level. In a series of well-planned and executed extended cruises and ocean races, George tested his vessel, his program, and himself in preparation for the great adventure that will unfold in the pages that follow.

In the late 1990s, having done his "homework," he raised the idea of *Brilliant's* millennium trip to Europe. George had lived and sailed there, and *Brilliant* had enough admirers among the cognoscenti to ensure her visit would be appreciated. Of course, there were hurdles to overcome. But from the time the trip was proposed it seemed like the right thing to do; so, one by one, the obstructions were addressed and dealt with. As time approached for the beginning of the voyage, George and those working with him had made all the appropriate preparations. *Brilliant* herself was ready in every way, adequate funds had been committed, every detail had been addressed, and Captain Moffett's dream was about to become a reality.

Few of us realized what a thrill it would be to follow the brilliant success of this voyage — through fair weather and foul — via modern communication technology. It is a gripping, suspenseful, funny, poignant, and triumphant tale. This publication makes it possible for us to relive this splendid adventure again and again.

J. Revell Carr
Director Emeritus, Mystic Seaport

Introduction

This narrative starts when we cast off to participate in Tall Ships races from Boston to Halifax, and then on to Amsterdam. It ends upon our return to Mystic Seaport after almost a year of superb sailing, which had passed too quickly. The full story begins, however, with years of planning and careful preparation that seemed eternally slow.

Back in 1985, after Brilliant's first return to Bermuda in 40 years, a few of us started thinking her historic 1933 sail to Europe should be relived. Off and on, this idea surfaced but it remained a fantasy. Our ability to reach out from our local waters was limited to programs in Maine, the Chesapeake, Bermuda, and Nova Scotia. Then, in 1997 the American Sail Training Association and the International Sail Training Association proposed a series of transatlantic races combined with spectacular harbor events, all as part of the millennium celebration. These events promised large gatherings of training vessels from all over the world.

Brilliant's participation seemed appropriate. Living the story of "what it means to go to sea" plays a dynamic role in our mission. The best way to know the ocean is to go there, and Brilliant has made that experience possible for thousands of people since becoming Mystic Seaport's sail-training vessel in 1953. An ocean passage would be merely an expansion of an existing program. So, we began to move from fantasy to con-

Introduction

crete planning.

Although *Brilliant* is an active sailing vessel, she is also an artifact in the collections of Mystic Seaport. Winning support to sail her to remote waters involved making a good argument that the journey would support the Museum's mission. We had to offer a viable financial plan, outline realistic logistics, and assess potential participant interest. Toward that end, *Brilliant* enthusiasts expressed readiness to provide financial assistance for both vessel preparation and scholarships. Experienced sailors came forward with logistical assistance, and from the very beginning, individuals showed eagerness to sail across the pond.

As in many successful operations, preparation involved many people. Museum staff, both paid and volunteer, gave generously of their time and enthusiasm. Long-standing donors sustained their support and new donors came forward. More than $100,000 was given to make the plan financially viable. Almost $40,000 in scholarships provided substantial support for 26 student sailors. Many of those who were so helpful are named in the acknowledgments that begin on the next page.

Brilliant's transatlantic adventure provided international exposure for Mystic Seaport and multilayered discovery for those who sailed. Showing a well-preserved and still active artifact in various European venues led to unusual exposure for the Museum. The journey's impact on our young sailors is evident in their own words, which appear on the pages of this book.

For many who go to sea, the experience is much more difficult than anything they could have imagined. Some don't make it back alive. Sadly, more will perish. Many of us have friends who have been lost with their ships, such as *Marques*, *Pride of Baltimore,* and *Albatross*. On this journey, *Brilliant* had better luck. We experienced some challenging weather, but it could have been much worse. We returned safely. And for that, we are most grateful.

Acknowledgements

Approval from Mystic Seaport's Executive Committee and the Board of Trustees was essential before we could commit time and energy to preparing a season of transatlantic sailing. A committee of advisors, including Frank Bohlen, Tom Cunliffe, Jim Giblin, Timmy Larr, Don Robinson, and Jon Wilson, was formed to help draft a concept that would achieve executive and trustee approval. Revell Carr, then President of Mystic Seaport, sustained his support throughout the process; all would have stalled without his commitment. Three other members of the Museum staff, Suzanne Reardon, Don Treworgy, and Ted Kaye, became heavily involved before and during the operation. Bookings, communications, and logistics hinged on their adding these tasks to already extensive workloads. Don devoted an enormous amount of time to receiving, recording, and forwarding the INMARSAT emails. The record that remains we owe to him.

In addition to serving on the "proposal committee," Frank Bohlen helped prepare the vessel's emergency gear and navigation kit. This included selecting about 100 charts — no small task. Frank also served as navigator/tactician or watch leader on the first two legs, spending six weeks aboard. His belief in the viability of the project proved encouraging when many had doubts. Jim Giblin also doubled his volunteer duties by taking on various engineering upgrades and navigating us

Acknowlegements

from New London to Boston.

Some volunteers have worked for years, coming in a day or two a week to help maintain the boat. As this unusual season approached, they increased their efforts to help us prepare. They include Don Boydon, Joe Birkle, Dick Inman, Brad Prohaska, Bob Redfern, Ed Seder, and Peter and Carol King.

Other Museum staff contributed in too many ways to list fully. Amy Hagberg, in her five years as mate, worked closely with volunteers to bring *Brilliant* to high standards of maintenance. Dean Seder fabricated, on short notice, various replacement parts. Lee Wacker, who had sailed aboard *Brilliant* as a teen student in 1993 and as cook in 1999, worked with intensity to prepare the ship's supplies, provision the galley, and build the offshore medical kit. She precisely anticipated her duties as medical officer and cook, and carried them out perfectly throughout her entire time aboard. Hannah Cunliffe, who served as cook on the challenging passages to and from Ireland, showed her spirited acceptance of the sea, gleaned from her wisdom after so many years of ocean travel as a young girl. Returning from Antigua via Bermuda led to difficult sailing, and both Laurie Belisle and Keith Chmura did a superb job of keeping us safe and fed.

Not enough can be said for Mate Christine Alberi's dedication in the hectic weeks before departure and during the stressful, sleepless time at sea. She, at the age of 24, led a watch on all six legs of the program, always eager for more responsibility. Students witnessed a skipper in the making. Also, she served as ship's photographer; we have her to thank for contributing so much to the record.

Volunteer watch leaders included Mary K. Bercaw Edwards and Rich King; both proved delights to have aboard. In Europe, Tom Cunliffe sailed with us to Ireland and then wrote about the passage in a lively article that appeared in a leading British publication. Sally McGee sailed with us from Ireland to Lisbon. None of us will forget her courage as she led a group out on the bowsprit to rescue a jib, adrift in a gale. Sally also set up our Web page, enabling many to discover our adventure.

Our donors made the transatlantic program possible. Some have supported the boat for decades, and others came forward with particular enthusiasm for this project. A boat of this age simply could not be trusted to take students to sea

Acknowlegements

unless a long history of careful maintenance set the foundation for "last minute" measures, such as a new suit of sails and a refastened bottom. Most donors prefer to remain anonymous; were we to list all, the page would be long. Those who have given and who are reading these words know we are grateful. The vast majority of students, 26 out of 36, could not have joined us without substantial financial help. Almost $40,000 of donated scholarships made this possible. This publication became possible through the generosity of three donors.

Even small books take a lot of work. Volunteer Laura Souhrada Kyle has given hundreds of hours to editing. Lorely Gaunt, who directs our product development, has worked well beyond the call of duty to make the presentation come together. Laura and Lorely have worked closely to produce this book.

The harbor events and international races were made possible by The American Sail Training Association and the International Sail Training Association, whose professional staff and hundreds of volunteers inspired thousands of trainees to reach beyond the expected. Five years of careful planning made it possible for vessels like *Brilliant* to take part in well-organized races and events.

Maynard and Anne Bray volunteered for the two-month winter watch in Antigua when the crew left for some time off before the start of the charter season. They were not content to only guard the boat, but also took on various maintenance projects.

Finally, we must remember the incredible hospitality that was shown in harbors everywhere we visited. In particular, we have Neil Simms to thank for setting up the reception given us by the Island Sailing Club in Cowes, England. Members of the Club who made this possible are acknowledged in the September entry, page 59. At Camper & Nicholsons in Gosport, England, we were given free dockage for both of our extended visits. In Ireland, we received free dockage from the Kinsale Yacht Club, thanks to Mick Loughnane who also offered support in our preparations for the passage to Portugal. In Antigua, we were given a substantial discount to enable us to stay at the marina dock, thanks to Carlo Franconi who, through his fine staff, also helped us run our successful winter charter season. When we arrived in Bermuda, we were

Acknowlegements

given free dockage at the Royal Bermuda Yacht Club, thanks to arrangements made by Joe Postich, who knows so much about the soul of wooden boats and the weaknesses of captains.

None know such weaknesses better than wives who endure long absences of distracted minds, not to mention distant bodies. Sabine knows me too well through her infinite patience and unlimited forgiveness.

A Note from the Editor

The first thing one notices about *Brilliant* is her classic beauty: her perfectly sculpted lines, the warmth of her wood, the gleam of her brass fittings. Those who know her well, however, love her for characteristics that are beyond skin-deep. She is strong, resilient, and takes the sea with power and grace. At 70-plus years of age, *Brilliant* remains precisely what her original owner wanted: a craft that's fast, weatherly, and as handsome as possible.

Yes, *Brilliant* has every reason to stand proud, but there was no reason to think she might trounce the entire fleet in the Tall Ships® 2000 transatlantic race.

Brilliant is a shrimp among tall ships. Her mainmast is only 80 feet high. She lacks the go-fast, high-tech materials of younger craft in the fleet. She had proven herself in a fast transatlantic passage only once before - setting a record generations ago, in 1933. The Tall Ships® 2000 fleet was handicapped to level the playing field, but few people expected *Brilliant* might win.

That's just what she did, however, with the help of her young crew, some dedicated instructors, and many enthusiastic supporters. Then she shifted gears and cruised the ports of Holland, England, Ireland, France, Spain, and Portugal before re-crossing the Atlantic, wintering in the Caribbean and finally turning north to her home: Mystic Seaport in Connecticut.

A Note from the Editor

It took almost a year to complete the journey.

Brilliant accommodates only about ten people. But that year she carried hundreds – perhaps thousands – of adventurers along for the ride, people who eagerly followed *Brilliant's* journey through dispatches emailed between Captain George Moffett and Don Treworgy, the ship's "point person" back at Mystic Seaport.

At first, the messages were a practical matter: through Treworgy, Moffett informed *Brilliant's* support team about logistic and operational needs. They were also a nice way to let family and friends know about the crew's well-being. So, Treworgy forwarded the messages to a few interested persons. Then the emails did what email does: they multiplied. The chain of recipients grew exponentially, and so did interest in *Brilliant's* adventure. Soon, Moffett's emails grew into a narrative of *Brilliant's* journey.

Moffett's way with words captivated armchair sailors. They could almost see the crew up to their waists on the bowsprit, struggling to secure a headsail; the frustrated cook, balancing a pot of hot stew with sea water slopping at her feet; the exhausted captain himself hunched over in the red, nighttime glow of the nav station, trying to type email and protect his keyboard from salt water at the same time.

In Moffett's original emails, Don Treworgy is a partner in dialogue. He is *Brilliant's* home messenger and an interpreter of events to subsequent readers. For the sake of narrative in this book, Treworgy fades into the background. But as the person who first put the emails into plain English (Moffett wrote in "shorthand" to cut satellite transmission costs), Treworgy was in fact the first editor of the material in this book. We wish to recognize him as such.

Laura Souhrada Kyle
Editor

ABOARD AN AMERICAN CLASSIC

Across the Atlantic with
BRILLIANT

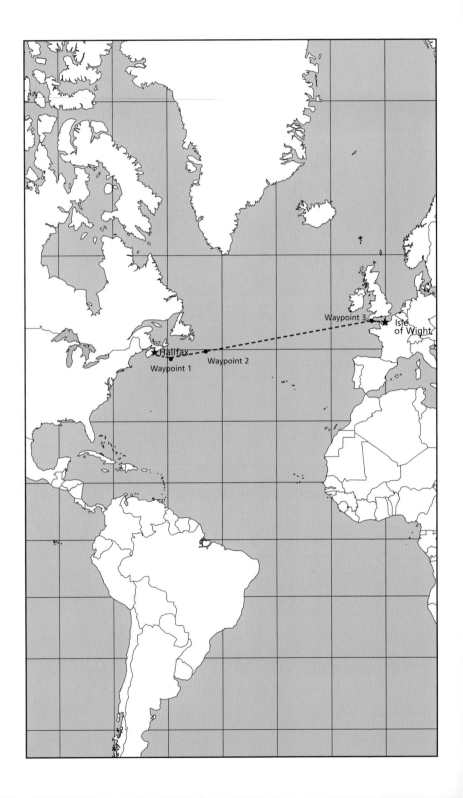

Chapter One

Among Tall Ships
July 14 - August 24, 2000

We set out to race ... outlast a calm enroute to Halifax ... survive gales and white water on the North Atlantic ... arrive victorious in England ... and enjoy the winner's spotlight in Amsterdam.

Friday July 14
Anchored in Buzzards Bay, MA, near the Cape Cod Canal entrance

Six cadets and four professional crew departed New London, CT, at 1132 Eastern Daylight Time on *Brilliant*, bound for Boston via the Cape Cod Canal. We had a speedy passage under sail, with speeds of 7 to 10 knots. We made it from Watch Hill to the canal in five hours and 40 minutes, on a close reach with favorable currents and winds at 15 to 20 knots. Soon after dark, we set anchor so the crew could sleep while awaiting a fair current through the canal.

After years of planning and preparation for this event, you might think nothing could go wrong in the final hours. But there's always the unexpected. Our 15-year-old single-side-band (SSB) radio needed repairs that went well into last night. We knew there was a problem with our INMARSAT-C satellite communications system but we had no diagnosis until this morning. It will have to be repaired in Boston before the

Crew List
July 14 - August 24
New London, CT to Amsterdam

Professional Crew

George Moffett, captain
Ledyard, CT

Christine Alberi, mate
Summit, NJ

Frank Bohlen, watch leader, weather and navigation specialist
Mystic, CT

Lee Wacker, cook and medical technician
Old Lyme, CT

Jim Giblin, navigator
Noank, CT
(New London to Boston leg only)

Cadets

Jonathan Feins
Rochester, NY

Matt Lincoln
Sherborn, MA

Katie Oman
Winchester, MA

Dan Parke
Syracuse, NY

Christopher Schmiedeskamp
Anchorage, AK

Myles Thurlow
West Tisbury, MA

"feeder" race to Halifax begins on Monday.

In every other way *Brilliant* lives up to her name, thanks to the hard work and commitment of Mystic Seaport's staff and friends. In the words of Walter Barnum, *Brilliant's* first owner, she's "as fast, weatherly and handsome as possible."

Sunday July 16
0758 EDT
Moored off Winthrop, MA (near Logan Airport)

We started through Cape Cod Canal at 0600 yesterday with a favorable current and reached Boston at 1430. Got some sleep yesterday afternoon and some this morning, but little or none last night. Squalls and high winds kept us busy because we're on a light mooring. There was a lot going on in the sky last night: we also saw fireworks above the harbor and the moon occasionally peeking out from behind the clouds.

In preparation for tomorrow's race, we put a double reef in the main sail and bent on the heavy weather jib. This was in part a drill, and would help make things less hectic in the morning. We anticipate a possible beat in winds of 25 to 31 mph, although 19 to 24 seems more likely. Southeasterly winds are forecast, with rain possible.

The race starts at 1615 EDT. We'll be in Class CI with *Jolie Brise*, winner of the very first Fastnet Race in 1925. *Jolie Brise* and *Brilliant* competed against each other in the 1932 Bermuda Race. That year, *Brilliant* nearly matched a course record. It'll be interesting to see how things play out in 2000!

Monday July 17
Current position: 42° 21′ N, 69° 26′ W
Making 8 knots on a course of 100° magnetic

Dense fog and the politics of Boston harbor control delayed our start. In the end, each vessel's starting time was taken as it crossed the line, which will make corrected time calculations very messy.

We sailed into a hole and suffered light air for three hours while the fleet sailed by. Now we're catching up in a 15-knot northwest wind; we anticipate the wind will go to the southwest.

Jolie Brise and Pride of Baltimore II are in sight but well to windward. We feel a bit of rivalry with Pride because one of her captains, Jan Miles, sailed four years as mate aboard Brilliant.

Tuesday July 18
Current position: 42° 28.5´ N, 68° 10.4´ W
Brazil Rock (the southern coast of Nova Scotia) is at 080° magnetic, 131 nautical miles distant

Our second day; our second hole. We sailed in and stood there (subject to current) for 13 hours – along with the rest of the fleet. There was much discussion among the boats about terminating the race because late arrival in Halifax would create problems. Many have already dropped out.

But now a light wind out of the south is giving us a beam-to close-reach with boat speeds ranging from 4 to 7 knots. The weather forecast suggests winds will go southwest at 10 to 15 knots.

Everyone aboard is in good spirits despite considerable frustration about the boat's rolling and sails' slatting through the night. No complaints about the food; Lee Wacker has been doing a great job with the meals. Likewise, Christine Alberi, Brilliant's mate, did a great job sailing her into way when light air came in at about 3 A.M.

Wednesday July 19
Current position: 43° 32´ N, 64° 11´ W
Making 7 knots on a heading of 050° magnetic; laying the finish line outside of Halifax Harbor, 62.7 nautical miles distant

Southwest winds of 17 to 27 knots gave us a broad reach around Cape Sable. We passed three miles south of Brazil Rock at 0255 EDT, making a good 10+ knots with fair current. A front with squalls and lightning moved over us as we approached the cape. So we shortened sail with a change of jib, lowered the fisherman and reefed the main – all under the glow of the moon seen through dense fog.

There's good visibility this morning for the second time

since leaving Boston in the fog, and we anticipate that it will continue; a northwest wind filled in at 0600. That wind is starting to go light, however. Twenty-five-knot winds have decreased to 11 to 16 knots and the seas are easing. We've already set our light-air canvas.

We're sure that we overtook some vessels last night and this morning, but don't know our current position in the fleet. Only one other vessel is in sight, and there are more than 40 in the fleet. A report yesterday said that we stood fifth in the fleet and second in our class. We think we're well ahead of *Jolie Brise*, whose captain wanted the race shortened so he and others could motor to Halifax, change crew, and prepare for the transatlantic race. That proposal became irrelevant when the wind filled in.

Thursday July 20
Halifax, Nova Scotia

Brilliant crossed the finish line ten miles outside of Halifax Harbor at 7:15:08 P.M. EDT with four square-riggers in sight. We sailed down the south coast in magnificent southwesterly winds shifting to northwesterly then returning to westerly, blowing 17 to 27 knots. It was a fast passage, often making more than 9 knots broad-reaching. Lots of tacking downwind with very busy gybing evolutions and jib changes as the wind eased and built. The crew have become very able at raising and lowering the fisherman staysail.

We think we were first over the finish line in our class and stand very well in the fleet, but won't know the results until the awards ceremony on Saturday, which takes place after a parade of all the ships' crews through the city. It's difficult to know our corrected time results; trying to determine the winner would be pure speculation.[1]

It took more than an hour after our finish to reach the inner harbor and take on fuel before proceeding to dock. All

---

1   *Brilliant's* time correction factor (or handicap) is about 0.6; the fastest boats rate somewhere around 1.0. *Brilliant's* corrected time is 0.6 of her elapsed racing time; about 40 percent of her real time is discounted. This theoretically allows a fair race between smaller vessels (40 feet long, for example) and much larger ones (some in this fleet are more than 300 feet).

was secured by midnight. Feeling mercy for the crew, this weakened captain allowed them to sleep in until 8 A.M., when – shamed by the very busy Italian crew aboard *Stella Polare* – we launched an intensive morning cleanup.

Stella is one of two Sparkman & Stephens 74-foot yawls built in 1965 for the Italian Naval Academy. Both have consistently taken naval cadets to sea since their delivery. *Stella Polare* is a beautifully built wooden vessel of the Italian yard Sangermani, Lavagna (near Genova). Two fine S&S designs (*Brilliant* being the other) lying side-by-side enhance the waterfront scene in this city, which is already jammed with beautiful boats, hundreds of thousands of visitors and more than 5,000 cadets.

Friday July 21
Halifax, Nova Scotia

An early report from the Race Committee indicates that on corrected time *Brilliant* came in four minutes behind *Jolie Brise*, even though *Brilliant* crossed the finish line some 25 nautical miles ahead. We made several mistakes which would account for this difference. The crew is enjoying shore leave; an unbelievable number of people are here to view the ships.

Saturday July 22
Halifax, Nova Scotia

Significant news! We just learned that some start and finish times got mixed up on reporting from different time zones: EDT and Greenwich Mean Time. We don't fully understand the details, but a recalculation has us beating *Jolie Brise* by one second! Yes, that is one second! The race director informed us a few minutes ago.

Brilliant is first in her class and third in fleet behind *Kaiwo Maru* and *Kruzenshtern*. The 90-year-old *Jolie Brise* sailed all the races coming over from Europe and we understand that she has been dominating Class CI, so she'll be happy to give up the burden of perpetual victory. Remember: she first competed with *Brilliant* in 1932.

The awards ceremony will be a big deal, preceded by a parade of some 5,000 cadets through the city and followed by parties for the crew and afterguard. Our youngest crew member, 17-year-old Myles Thurlow, and I will sit at the front of the audience to receive *Brilliant's* award.

Olin Stephens may be happy to hear his *Stella Polare* took second in Class CIII, the go-fast, spinnaker-flying sail-training vessels. She is crewed by very friendly and intense cadets from the Italian Naval Academy. *Pride of Baltimore*, with captain Jan Miles who was a mate on *Brilliant*, placed second in Class B and ninth in fleet. She too will be racing to Amsterdam. Thirty boats finished the race; 28 did not for a variety of reasons, but primarily due to long periods of light air sandwiched between 17 to 27 knot winds. The crew is touring the harbor now after cleaning the vessel and playing cards.

Sunday July 23
Halifax, Nova Scotia

Yesterday's awards ceremony was elegant. Five thousand cadets, accompanied by drummers and marching bands, paraded from Pier 21 through town and up to the inner courtyard of Halifax's Citadel. An estimated 100,000 to 150,000 visitors lined the parade route. *Brilliant* received awards for first place in Class CI and best corrected time for a North American vessel.

Now it's back to business. We attended a two-hour meeting today to prepare for the transatlantic race, review weather conditions, and discuss safety issues. *Brilliant's* crew has been drilled on safety and setting the storm trysail. Participants are required to "round" three waypoints, but there are no physical marks at any of these roundings. Two of them are positioned to keep the fleet south of the shallow water and possible ice on the Grand Banks. The third is just off Bishop Rock, Scilly Isles, southwest of England's Land's End.

A spreader light had to be secured, and Christine did a fine job of installing the new unit. We've been taking on provisions and water; Lee is now preparing dinner. We cast off from the dock at 0730 EDT (1130 GMT) tomorrow; the race starts at 1300 EDT (1700 GMT).

The city of Halifax has been gracious to us, but we're ready for the peace of the open sea and the challenge of the race. We'll email daily reports around midday local ship time, unless conditions and sail handling necessitate a delay.

Monday July 24
0829 EDT
Halifax, Nova Scotia

We've just cast off our lines and are waiting to join a parade of ships, which will make a two-hour loop of the harbor before going to the race starting area. It's a spectacular sight as the ships back out of their dock locations – there are many Class A ships and a number of them are more than 300 feet long. The five thousand cadets are now ready for sea again. Halifax claims this is the largest gathering of sailing ships since the Spanish Armada!

The entire event has been extremely well organized and on an especially well-suited waterfront, where one could stroll along a boardwalk past all of the docked vessels. We've had a banner with Mystic Seaport's Web address flying between our masts; it will be interesting to learn if there are many new hits on the *Brilliant* section of the Web site. All times that I mention from now on will be GMT as we have shifted ship's time to GMT for the race. Our start time today is 1720 GMT (1320 EDT).

Tuesday July 25
Current position: 43° 43′ N, 61° 31′ W
About 79 miles from waypoint #1, which bears 143° magnetic
Making 4.6 knots

The transatlantic race started on time yesterday, south of Halifax Harbor. The Class A and B vessels crossed the line before our class, creating a spectacle none of us will forget: 18 ships clustered at the starting line, all under full sail illuminated by bright sunlight.

We started at 1730 GMT (1330 EDT) with light south-

southwest winds. We overtook all in our class and two hours later overtook *Pride of Baltimore II* which was leading Class B. We passed the 375-foot *Kruzenshtern* in daylight and in the night overtook *Mir*, which was leading the Class A ships. Just ahead of us at this time are some of the go-fast Class CIIs and the very fast S&S-designed *Stella Polare* of spinnaker Class CIII.[2] All others are out of sight astern, but visibility has dropped so we can't tell how narrow our lead may be. Radar suggests we are doing well in the light air: we see no targets within 15 nautical miles. *Mir* appears on radar to be about 17 nautical miles to our lee. We think she'll have trouble fetching the first weather waypoint at 43° N, 60° W.

There's a deepening low pressure area ahead. Through the night we were able to make good our course (with some help from currents) but now the winds have backed,[3] forcing us onto a heading of 125° magnetic when we need 143°. It looks like a tack will be necessary to fetch the waypoint. The second waypoint may not be such a problem because it's more to the east, at 42° N, 50° W.

If we sail into the low, it will give us more – if not too much – wind. But that's more than a day away. For now, we're close-reaching in light air. It's slow going, but to our advantage; the big square-riggers really take off when broad-reaching in strong air.

We whispered by virtually the entire fleet yesterday; *Jolie Brise* is probably more than 20 nautical miles astern. We're doing lots of careful sail trim, using flashlights at night so we can see the telltales and windsock; it's intensive work in the dark.

Now a few words from crew member Chris Schmiedeskamp:

---

2 In fact, *N. V. Hamburg*, a class CIII modern racing sloop, was also ahead.

3 Winds are partly caused by differences in air pressure: air from a high-pressure area will flow into an area that has less pressure. Many factors affect wind strength, but in general the greater the pressure difference between zones, the stronger the wind. In the Northern Hemisphere, wind blows counterclockwise around a low and clockwise around a high. When wind shifts in a counterclockwise direction, it is called a "backing" wind. When it moves clockwise, it is "veering."

"Good Morning! Pilot whales have made this watch interesting so far, but we need more wind. Calm seas are the conditions of the hour, and we would all like to get a little more way on. Greetings to all our friends on land!"

Wednesday July 26
1337 GMT (0937 EDT)
Current position: 77 nautical miles southeast of Sable Island
Speed of 9 knots, making good a course of 140° magnetic
Position at 1200 GMT (0800 EDT): 42° 51′ N, 59° 09′ W on a course of 120° magnetic (100° true)

We rounded waypoint #1 at 1200 GMT (0400 EDT). Most of the fleet has not yet rounded. Ahead of us by a few miles are *Stella Polare*, *Maiden* (a modern sloop), and *Esprit* (a modern schooner from Germany). All others are more than 30 nautical miles astern, including *Pride of Baltimore II* and *Jolie Brise*.

However, we're now in stronger wind and many in the fleet will soon catch up. The wind is blowing from the east-northeast at 20 knots, and we are close-reaching to keep moving through the growing seas. We shortened sail just after rounding waypoint #1, putting a single reef in the main and putting up the #2 jib. With the foresail, it's enough canvas to drive us along. Our course to the next waypoint (42° N, 50° W) is 114° magnetic but we can only fetch 135° with the wind and seas. It's very hard to move around on the boat now compared with the relative ease of the last 2 days.

We have a three-watch system going to give everyone as much rest as possible. We used a two-watch system on the Boston-to-Halifax leg. On that leg, Frank Bohlen, a professor of marine sciences at the University of Connecticut and a Mystic Seaport trustee, did a great job as a navigator, tactician, and weather specialist. Now Frank is also leading one of the watches. Christine and I are leading the other two.

... later, July 26
Current position: 42° 33′ N, 58° 04′ W
Approximately 2,467 miles to the finish line, south of England's Isle of Wight

The boat is moving well but there's some seasickness among the crew. This is no longer smooth sailing.

Around noon daily, every boat in the fleet radios its position to the race organizers. We didn't hear the standings today but think we're leading our class on corrected time. We should be doing well against the entire fleet, because all of the "big boys" have to give us time. Furthermore, in the light air we gained a lead of more than 50 nautical miles.

Now we're riding the southeast side of a big high, which gives us these east-northeast winds of about 20 knots – almost twice the strength forecast. There's a low pressure system 300 miles east of us, but we doubt that we'll catch it unless it stalls or moves very slowly. If we do catch it, we hope our present course will sail us to its south side for fair winds.

We just enjoyed anther superb dinner cooked by Lee in the leaping galley.

Thursday July 27
1602 GMT (1202 EDT)
Position at 1200 GMT (0800 EDT): 41° 51′ N, 55° 19′ W
Nautical miles to the finish: 2,297

High pressure continues to give us 15-to 20-knot winds from the east-northeast, pushing us along at 8+ knots. We're still under reefed main, full foresail, and #2 jib; the seas are lumpy and irregular from (we think) Gulf Stream eddies. Frank's knowledge about the Gulf Stream has been very useful.

We're sailing conservatively because the ride is very uncomfortable when we push the boat harder into the wind. Close-reaching is a good compromise between speed and comfort. Some boats have sailed much further off the wind than *Brilliant* and one or two modern ones are upwind of us.

We had a lot of white water on deck through the night and I went completely underwater when I went forward to secure

some lines in the early-morning hours. The crew is generally
soaked and enjoying off-watch with their eyes firmly closed.
The cook is also soaked because a leaky mast boot lets water
from the deck into the galley below.

We're still first in class and first in fleet on corrected time,
according to today's reports. Long-time competitor *Jolie Brise* is
second in class, fifth in fleet, and about 150 miles astern and
to leeward of us. *Pride of Baltimore II*, with Jan Miles aboard, is
first in her class, seventh in fleet, and about 100 miles astern
and to leeward. *Stella Polare* is 13 miles ahead of us but much
to our surprise, 25 miles to leeward. Is she playing the anticipated low? Or does her crew of Italian naval cadets prefer a
more horizontal platform for their espresso?

Now a few words from crew member Dan Parke:

"Ever since we switched the ship clocks to GMT, daylight,
sleep, and meals seem to come at arbitrary times. The three-
team watch cycle is an improvement over the schedule we
used between Boston and Halifax, but since more people are
off-watch at the same time it takes creativity to find a leeward
bunk. Some have taken to resting on the floor, wedged
between the dining table and the windward settee. Meals
sometimes come during sleep time, but are always worth
waking up for."

Friday July 28
1355 GMT (0955 EDT)
Position at (1200 GMT) 0800 EDT: 40° 54′ N, 51° 42′ W
Nautical miles to finish line: approximately 2,160
Elapsed race time: 3 days, 18.5 hours
Average speed since the start: 6.25 knots

Fleet position reports are just in, along with a weather
forecast from Herb Hilgenberg.[4] Frank uses computer software
to combine Herb's radioed forecast with weather information

---

4   Herb Hilgenberg, an amateur meteorologist, provides excellent weather
analysis and guidance, free of charge, for ships in the Atlantic Ocean,
Caribbean and Gulf of Mexico. He broadcasts by SSB radio daily from his home
in Ontario, Canada. He agreed to act as meteorologist for the entire racing
fleet. His reports were received by *Mir*, a three-masted Class A Russian ship,
whose crew would simplify and rebroadcast the information each day.

that we receive by fax. We're still positioned well ahead in our class; on corrected time we may still be first in fleet. We caught up with the S&S design, *Stella Polare*, by reaching down on her. She was well to our lee yesterday and is now about two miles to weather. Otherwise, there are no boats in sight and according to the reports, many are hundreds of miles astern.

We're sailing well south of the second waypoint and we're comfortable with that. We think this course will put us safely on the south side of the anticipated deepening low to our east. Otherwise we could encounter gale-force winds on our nose in the northern sectors; we'd prefer favorable winds of less strength in the southern sectors. Frank is keeping an ear to the weather reports.

This is still a couple of days down the track. For now we're enjoying east-northeast winds at about 20 knots and often we are making speeds of more than 8 knots. Reaching off to take the seas at an easier angle this morning gave us speeds of 9.9 knots over the bottom. That's an average taken from our Global Positioning System. Our water speed isn't as reliable as the GPS, but we do use it to judge relative speed when trimming the sails.

Lots of water on deck at times, even as we reach off. A single-reefed main, foresail, and #2 jib continue to do the job, but if it builds we'll shorten to double-reefed main, fore, forestaysail, and #3. Moving about with the boat on her ear makes us reflect on the comforts of home. We're all ready for some broader reaching.

Now some words from our cook, Lee Wacker:

"I'm happier now because George has stopped the waterfalls that have been pouring down my back at unexpected moments. The drenching kept me lively but life will be better without it. I've been faring well in the galley even though we are so heeled over, but I do wish that people would eat a little more. I don't want to be accused of not feeding them! We still have plenty of stores including mini-marshmallows and Nutella, so I think we'll survive a while longer."

Why is it so wet on deck?
The really large seas in an offshore gale are actually long swells – a
boat rises and falls smoothly with those, until the storm gets so
strong that breakers build on top of the swells. It's the smaller
waves on top of the swells that cause most of the discomfort, putting white water on deck – and permeating below.

... later July 28
2345 GMT (1945 EDT)

A bit of evening quiet time and easier seas enable me to
work this delicate laptop and send off a note. I'd planned to
send messages at noon GMT daily, but the nav station is rather
busy at that time, receiving weather reports and fleet positions, and the cabin crowded with crew changing watch.

Everyone has been saying how nice it is to move around
the boat without her plunging into seas. We're still heeled over
– about 15° with some sea action – but it's now possible to
wash, use the head, cook, clean, and perform other duties
without holding on for dear life. Imagine the gyrations of a
person attempting to use the head in rough conditions; it can
take half an hour to take your pants down without breaking
an arm!

... still later July 28

The wind has freshened again, but we're making only 8
knots with the fisherman down and a full main. We're all concerned about the low pressure that is forecast to reach us in a
couple of days. At what latitude will its center be? We can only
guess.

We're much further south than anticipated because of the
persistent, large high pressure. Fortunately for us, other vessels – including *Pride of Baltimore* – have been forced even further south; they had to reach off even more than we to cope
with the seas. *Jolie Brise* had a lot of difficulty with the seas and
is now 170 nautical miles astern. *Stella Polare* has been with us
the entire day but is slowly pulling away, especially now that

we have taken in the fisherman. We'd get about another half knot of speed with the fisherman, but we'd be slightly over-canvassed and uncomfortable in the gusts.

The conditions are taking their toll on the crew. One has suffered several days of seasickness. We were becoming a little worried but all is better now, and both food and fluid have reached his tender tissues. Another fell today while taking in the fisherman and bruised his ribs pretty badly but nothing is broken. Soon we'll be where rescue or evacuation is slow at best, so we're emphasizing the need for caution – especially when moving about on deck.

We learned earlier that we are still first in fleet and class on corrected time. That's hard for us to believe because it feels like we are going so slowly. All is relative.

Saturday July 29
1616 GMT (1216 EDT)
Position at 1200 GMT (0800 EDT): 39° 55′ N, 48° 07′ W
Making 6 knots

We've been holding port tack with good speed for days. But a few hours ago we tacked onto starboard to sail north, making 030° to 040° magnetic – a heading that is nearer the "great circle" course to England (077°) than we'd make on port. *Stella Polare* went to starboard with us for a while but then back to port, perhaps to stay south or perhaps for the kinder sea slant.

Studying various forecasts, we've concluded that port tack was taking us too far south to glean the benefits still available from the high to the north and to get the best of the predicted low coming east from the Maritimes. Herb Hilgenberg thinks vessels in latitudes north of 44° risk being on the north side of the low and getting gale-force winds. But the weather fax from the Marine Prediction Center shows the low tracking farther north than Herb predicts. If we can benefit from the south side, we'll have 20 to 25 knots from the south or southwest. We don't want to miss the helpful winds, hence our decision to tack north. Frank has been leading our discussions about the weather.

I discussed this yesterday with Jan Miles of *Pride of Baltimore II*. At that time he intended to stay south of 40° but we haven't discussed it since. The low will reach *Pride of Baltimore* and the other boats before it hits *Brilliant*, so they'll close the gap of our lead if our thoughts about the low's movement and location prove true. We are now about 240 nautical miles ahead of *Pride* and even further ahead of *Jolie Brise* after a very fast night.

We've set full canvas, including the #1 jib for light air, which is currently out of the east, and have just enough power to push through these gentle swells and light seas. If we progress well through the afternoon and evening, we'll tack somewhere after 41° N.

The Azores are temptingly close: the crew suggested we bag the race and take a few days of island life before pushing on to Amsterdam. This was just after they cleaned up the personal gear strewn all over the ship and washed layers of salt off the deck.

Now a few words from ship's mate Christine Alberi:

"The ship has finally calmed enough for us to dust off our sextants and take some sights. We hope to have a running fix by afternoon. Myles is using the student sextant from Mystic Seaport's Planetarium for his first offshore sights. Chris, Jon, and I enjoyed a fantastic dawn watch in which we saw incredible stars, phosphorescence, a sliver of the waning moon, and watched the sunrise. To top it off, we passed *Stella Polare* and then had Lee's fabulous breakfast burritos! The crew's becoming expert at sailing the boat and sensing shifts in the wind and seas. It makes life easier for watch officers."

... later, July 29
1854 GMT (1454 EDT)
Current position: 40° 22.5´ N, 47° 41.9´ W

We've found the core of the Gulf Stream again by using the GPS to watch our course over the bottom and are gaining a 20° lift into the wind. This puts us on track for the great circle route to England. We know it's a momentary pleasure; we'll tack later when we detect that we're sailing out of the stream.

Sunday July 30

Position at 1200 GMT (0800 EDT): 41° 27′ N, 46° 36′ W
Making good a course of 078° magnetic
Boat speed: 8 knots
Elapsed time since the start: 5 days, 18 hours
Nautical miles to the finish: 1,943

Pride of Baltimore II is gaining on us, narrowing our lead to 120 nautical miles. With stronger winds on a reach she will catch us. *Jolie Brise* is now 210 nautical miles astern. Two ships have retired from the race, leaving a fleet of 36 ships – 26 of which are still west of 50° longitude! *Stella Polare* is the closest boat to us, 25 miles to our southeast after we split tacks yesterday.

We decided to keep to the north because weather predictions call for the low pressure area to track east or northeast (rather than southeast) and, according to Herb, turn into a double-center low. No one on board is certain about Herb's use of the term "double-center low."[5] We wonder if he might be referring to a "secondary low."[6]

I've come to have a deep respect for secondary lows. Fifteen sailors died in the 1979 Fastnet Race, in part because they were hit by a secondary low in a region with shallows and dangerous currents. Years ago, while sailing my own boat in the English Channel, I found myself in serious trouble because of a fast-moving secondary low.

It's also not clear if we'll sail into a weakening high before the low catches us. The seas have not yet picked up and we're enjoying southeast winds of 15 to 20 knots on the west side of the high.

Strong winds still threaten if we get too far north; we just heard of boats to the northwest of us being hit by violent squalls with heavy rain and winds up to 40 knots. We've already struck the #1 jib, put up the smaller #2, and bent on

---

5 A double-center low occurs when one low catches up with another to create an oblong low-pressure area, charted with an L at both ends. The two can merge to form one low, which usually covers a larger area, but is not necessarily more powerful or more dangerous.

6 A secondary low is one that spins off from a primary low-pressure system. These are known for being dangerous and fast-forming. They occur more often in the northeast Atlantic than in the west, particularly in the latitudes near Ireland and England.

the #3 heavy weather jib to reduce the amount of hectic activity later. There will be water everywhere. The crew is well-drilled in reefing the main. My guess is that we'll be well shortened-down late tonight.

We all hope the low stays north; you can be sure the fleet's smaller boats are watching it with considerable anxiety and the bigger boats with great hope.

Monday July 31
1447 GMT (1047 EDT)
Current position: 42° 41´ N, 42° 31´ W
Elapsed time since the start: 6 days, 15 hours
Distance to the finish: 1,757 nautical miles

The latest forecast suggests that our position will keep us on the safe side of the low, just south of the center. We are sailing east to hold our latitude although we'd be much more comfortable and sail much faster at the "great circle" heading for England (080° magnetic or 060° true). *Pride of Baltimore II* is hove to because she can't hold a course that's east enough to maintain her latitude; she doesn't want to risk being further north.

The gale-force winds forecast for our area of the high haven't materialized. Still, all night we've had 25- to 30-knot winds and lumpy seas with related pitching – conditions we'll have to live with, because to slow our northing we must stay close hauled to the wind and seas. Even if we end up in the worst of the forecast low, it won't be too serious: forecasters are now talking only 40-knot winds and we've prepared by shortening down to heavy-weather jib, forestaysail, fore, and single-reefed main.

... later, July 31

We're talking about putting a second reef in the main; always a sign that it should be in already. Our next step, if the winds hit 40 knots, would be to drop the heavy weather #3 and sail without a jib, under the double-reefed main, fore, and forestaysail. Twice on other trips we had sustained winds of 40 knots (gusting higher) and it wasn't uncomfortable sailing on a broad reach. This low shouldn't be a significant threat unless it comes with serious squalls.

Oops! The wind has just freshened to more than 30 knots so we are REALLY getting serious about that second reef. Just going on deck now to take in a tuck.

... still later, July 31

Done! And we dropped the #3 so we're ready for a lot more wind than we currently have, but maybe this sail configuration will give us some quiet and enable the crew (myself included) to get some sleep. I've had three hours in the last 24, what with all the sail changes, weather discussions, and lively pitching about. I've been so tired, I nodded off making a log entry last night.

At this moment we're still reaching off while the crew secures the #3 to the bowsprit. Any sail on deck must be lashed down securely, otherwise the seas could take charge and make more work for us later. We also reached off to charge the batteries and refrigeration because the engine isn't happy with these steep angles and all the pitching. Reaching off isn't a problem, but it moves us north where we don't want to be. In fact, it has taken us 12 miles north in the last few hours.

When we reach off it's like a mill pond; when we come back onto the wind, it's a howling tempest – white water everywhere. This should all be behind us in 48 hours so we need merely hold on a bit longer.

Below, the boat looks like the aftermath of an undisciplined slumber party, with bedding and clothing all about. The three-watch system doesn't allow us to have our own bunks, so we are "hot-bunking." We each have to move our bedding and pillows with us to our next, new bunk. One person sleeps on the main cabin sole because no one wants to sleep in the fo'c'sle, where we normally have four bunks. Brilliant is set up for six sea berths with lee rails; this is the compromise we must make to get the added rest in a three-watch system (assuming that one's off-watch hours aren't interrupted by sail changes or emergencies).

We're now sailing comfortably, making 8.5 knots and a course made good of 110° magnetic (090° true). I'm off to find a hot bunk.

... still later, July 31
2131 GMT (1731 EDT)
Making 8+ knots on a course of 100° magnetic (about 070° true)

We just enjoyed another great meal which Lee created under adverse circumstances. Imagine preparing a dinner for ten in a kitchen that's moving up and down several feet with irregularity and occasionally lurching to the side as the boat slides off a wave. At the same time, imagine that someone keeps dumping water on the floor where you stand holding onto a pan of hot whatever. If you can imagine all this, you might get an idea of Lee's situation.

Unfortunately the mast boot, which should stop leaks around the mast (and in *Brilliant's* case, into the galley), is leaking big time. Salt water is getting all over the floor, all over Lee, leaking onto the icebox doors and into the icebox itself. Some food has already spoiled. Lee bailed out the icebox this afternoon and set up a plastic curtain to keep water out. We can't fix the mast boot until we are in calmer waters.

Our onboard weather and navigation specialist, Frank Bohlen, has been doing a superb job keeping track of the weather faxes. We've been painfully reminded that meteorology remains an imprecise science. Projections of this low's movement have changed so often that navigational decisions are best-guess judgments.

We're still enjoying about 30 knots out of the southeast. We anticipate the first part of the low will hit us tonight. The barometer is dropping very slowly. It's now at 30.28 inches and was 30.38 last night. We think we see a squall line ahead so may soon be shortening sail by taking in the main.

Tuesday August 1
1659 GMT (1259 EDT)
Current position: 43° 15´ N, 37° 27´ W
Position as of 1:00 pm EDT: About 360 nautical miles northwest of Flores in the Azores

We're in the good stuff (heavy winds and seas) now. It has been blowing over 30 knots, with more to come. The seas are up to 15 feet and sometimes come aggressively on deck. For hours the Gulf Stream has helped us with an extra knot of speed. Often we're making a speed of 10 knots over the bottom. The wind has just moderated to a little under 30 knots, but we are keeping our storm trysail, fore, and forestaysail set, as we have since early this morning when the winds freshened with gusts of 40 knots. We're still under the influence of high pressure but expect the low will dominate our lives tomorrow.

Herb, the fleet meteorologist, advises that winds will be 20 to 25 knots south of latitude 44°, but to the north, a gale. So we're easting again, to minimize the struggle tomorrow. We sailed through the night in rain that was often heavy and winds gusting to 40 knots; steady winds were 25 to 30 knots. *Brilliant* handled it very well under shortened sail. With our present configuration, including the storm trysail, we can take a lot. The crew are tired but in good spirits and are willing to do difficult sail changes – even with the elements in their faces.

A big systems failure has us concerned: no gas is reaching the stove. I suspect a faulty gas regulator or solenoid valve. We're also having trouble with the watermaker. It worked fine at slower speeds but when we sail fast, air gets into the system and we have to shut down and bleed it. Yesterday our angle of heel and our speed made it impossible to bleed the system. We anticipate light air ahead, so think we can solve this problem. Unfortunately we have no spares aboard to fix the stove gas problem.

Today's report indicates we are still first in class and fleet but the 310-foot *Mir* sailed by in the night, probably making 15 knots or more. She already stands second in the fleet and first in the square-rigged class, so we expect with these gale winds she'll be leading by tomorrow on corrected as well as elapsed time. *Pride of Baltimore II* is still well behind us but she too will take off when these strong winds blow on her quarter. I'm in daily contact with *Pride's* Jan Miles, comparing conditions and expectations.

Wednesday August 2
1700 GMT (1300 EDT)
Current position: 44° 17′ N, 32° 59′ W
Heading: 080° magnetic, on the "great circle" course for England
Distance to waypoint #3 (Bishop Rock): 1,123 nautical miles
Position at 1200 GMT (0800 EDT): 43° 59′ N, 33° 47′ W on a course of
* 060° true, speed of 9 knots*

Our cook is somewhat happier because the stove is breathing gas again but waterfalls are still cascading down the mast. We can't fix that until we slow down and have calmer seas. The stove problem was a faulty solenoid, not the regulator.

We had a rather rough night with gale winds (34 to 47 knots) and heavy, driving rain. We shortened down to only the storm trysail and forestaysail and made a steady 9+ knots, with a great reach across the growing seas. Taking in the foresail at night in a gale was good experience. We began adding sail this morning: first a reefed foresail and then the heavy-weather jib. We're still using the storm trysail and holding 9+ knots. Carrying four small patches of sail low to the deck creates great speed with low heel. The helm is surprisingly light because of the small sail area aft. We're almost upright and roaring along on a broad reach. We could take in the storm trysail now and reset the double-reefed main to make another 0.1 knot but we'd pay the price in more heel and a harder helm.

Frank received encouraging weather information this morning which suggests that we just brushed the east side of the low and have sailed back into the high on its northwest side. The barometer hit its low during last night's rain and high winds but has come up again. We may ride the high and get its winds of 25+ knots for another day or two.

With the wind on our quarter, life is much better. The smoother sailing has allowed us some sleep so we're all feeling good. Sea life is easier to spot in smoother water. We've seen many whales and came upon a pod of sleeping pilot whales. Porpoises have done their thing, diving off our bow. Two sea turtles and a "giant" jellyfish were spotted recently, even among the waves.

Brilliant is in great shape. I'm always amazed at her sea-kindly motion and how well she responds to the right combination of sails. She is indeed a great design for ocean voyaging, very comfortable and fast relative to most of the fleet – even in light air. And now, in fresher air, we're still holding our position of first in class, first in fleet (corrected time). We've logged a couple of 200-plus-mile days in this heavy stuff. Remember, this is the same *Brilliant* that for nine days in a row averaged 200 miles, making it from Nantucket Light to Bishop Rock in just 15 days, on her first transatlantic crossing in 1933. All of us now have a sense of what it takes to keep a boat moving for such a fast passage.

Thursday August 3
1706 GMT (1306 EDT)
Position at 1200 GMT (0800 EDT): 45° 33´ N, 29° 15´ W
Making 9 knots on a course of 075° magnetic

We have bright sunlight and fair breezes of 20 knots on our quarter as we ride up the northwest side of the high that has been so kind to us. The entire crew emerged like rats from a soaking-wet hole to lie on deck and have a field day cleaning, airing, and fixing various aggravations such as the leaky mast boot. The stove is working fine and we made some water today; there's much less anxiety.

Spirits are so high that we're having a party to celebrate being more than halfway across – even though the actual event was quite a while ago. At this moment, we're 1,890 nautical miles from Mystic and only 904 nautical miles from Bishop Rock. Balloons and party decor have appeared in the main cabin and Lee, the wonder cook, has put together some special fixings. The boat smells much better now that it has been aired. The feeling of being hunkered down in survival mode is just a memory.

We're still holding first in class and fleet but feel certain that one of the big square-rigs will take over soon. *Dar*

Mlodziezy (300+ feet long) sailed 310 miles in 24 hours with the benefit of the gales. *Mir* is hundreds of miles ahead, probably making speeds near 12 to 15 knots. We have the satisfaction of knowing *Pride of Baltimore II* (with Captain Jan Miles) is 188 miles to our west and that the Italian Navy's S&S-designed *Stella Polare* is some 400+ miles astern.

... later, August 3
2031 GMT (1631 EDT)

A few words from crew member Dan Parke:
"Standing on the bowsprit with surprisingly warm mid-Atlantic water up to one's waist is a strange place for an epiphany, but that was exactly my position when I realized this may be my last summer vacation. Then Myles Thurlow tugged on the jib and passed me another few feet of luff, and we got the sail changed. That was the first sail change of a series that would see us shorten all the way down to a storm trysail and forestaysail and then back to full canvas. The past few days have been a trial of stamina, concentration, and teamwork. Squalls with cold rain and wind, seas slapping the hull and drenching the watch on deck; after four hours we'd go below, shed our foul weather gear, and find a roughly horizontal surface to collapse on. The off-watches are looking forward to sleeping in a clean and ventilated cabin."

Friday August 4
1514 GMT (1114 EDT)
Position at 1200 GMT position: 47° 20′ N, 24° 51′ W
Making 8.5 knots on a course of 080° magnetic (065° True)

Today we marked our best noon-to-noon run thus far: 217 nautical miles, giving us a seven-day running average of 206 nautical miles! Our friend Jan Miles on *Pride of Baltimore II*, about 188 nautical miles to our west, says they also had their best daily run; 239 nautical miles, which narrows the gap between us.

We are flying light air canvas (#1, foresail, fisherman, mainsail), with the apparent wind just abaft of the beam, blowing 15 to 18 knots. Our worry now is the big high-pressure area to our southeast, which could move far enough north to keep us from the desired easterly component of our course. We are sliding around the 1034 millibar contour of the high pressure center, which is at 45° N, 20° W.

Now some insights from specialist Frank Bohlen:

"The weather patterns have been relatively unusual the past 10 days. The normal west to east migration of systems has been disrupted by a slow north/south migration. High and low pressure systems develop and then remain nearly stationary before dissipating. This has created some interesting navigational challenges. We've been fortunate to be able to take advantage of most circumstances so far; a tribute to Brilliant's sailing abilities.

"Our current challenge: a stationary high pressure area between us and the finish. We've been relying on the U.S. weather faxes to study our options but are limited to a single transmission each day, so we spend a lot of time watching the barometer; real high tech!" Now crew member Katie Oman:

"We are very, very happy to be dry and warm, and are still busy cleaning up the boat and ourselves. For the first time in a week, some of us are actually awake when off watch. We're getting involved in the likes of Harry Potter, of which there is one copy on board. We're all looking forward to our eventual landfall in England, but no one dares to say when that might be."

Saturday August 5
1628 GMT (1228 EDT)
Position at 1200 GMT: 48° 11′ N, 21° 00′ W
Distance to Bishop Rock: 546 nautical miles
Distance to Portsmouth, England: 780 nautical miles

Jon, Frank, and I composed a long message today. Then, when I attempted to fix a computer glitch, I eliminated the message. It's very frustrating because there's a lot of good stuff to report. I've lost heart for now, so I'll just report the basics and call it a day.

We are sailing in light air making only 6 knots but hoping conditions will enable us to close the gap a little with Russia's

Mir, which is about 85 miles ahead. Smooth sailing and bright sun has the crew in high spirits. We made lots of water today, so crew members are talking about washing their hair. The audacity!

Sunday August 6
0701 GMT (0301 EDT)
Position at 0645 GMT (0245 EDT): 48° 29′ N, 18° 46′ W
Boat speed of 5.8 knots, making good a course of 095° magnetic
     (083° true)

This has been a long, difficult night: two knots of wind with light swells rolling the boat just enough to knock the feeble wind out of the sails and frustrate us with the slatting sound and the thought that we could be caught in the core of the high for days. None of us are keen to re-live the lack of wind and the waiting that characterized much of the Boston-to-Halifax race. We'll know at noon how the fleet fared overnight but anticipate that because we're ahead and sailed into the high early, the rest of the fleet will have stronger winds and catch up with us, as *Pride of Baltimore II* has done over the past 48 hours.

Even this doesn't quell the enthusiasm of this crew. They're now into the rhythm of standing watch, reading, sleeping, chatting, and listening to daily performances of Harry Potter, dramatically delivered by Dan, the man of many voices.

In the middle of the night a pod of dolphins raced over to join us and could be seen coming from a distance like illuminated torpedoes. The water here is rich in microscopic life and the phosphorescence seems exceptionally strong. Our hands glow when we scoop water out of a bucket.

Our current course is a little high from the desired one of 089° magnetic but necessary to produce enough apparent wind to keep *Brilliant* moving. This is very difficult to endure when we've been spoiled by continuous 9-knot runs and days of 200+ nautical miles. We want out of this high.

Monday August 7
1335 GMT (0935 EDT)
Position at 1200 GMT (0800 EDT): 48° 32′ W, 16° 23′ W
Making 6 knots on a course of 090° to 110° magnetic
Distance to Bishop Rock: 395 nautical miles

A day of frustration, a night of torment. Why do we do this? What's the point? How foolish to be ocean racing, when days of hard sailing are consumed by a day of calm. How foul can one's mood become with perpetual slatting, whap-snap, whap-snap – all through the darkness?

Things are a little better now, with a light breeze that's sufficient to push us along, but our second-worst fear – that of sailing into the dead hole of the high – became reality shortly before sunset. We knew most of the fleet astern still had good air, making up to 9.5 knots, to decrease our lead. *Pride of Baltimore II* is now ten miles ahead of us. She held to the west and north to ride the outside edge of the 1028 millibar isobar and so kept speed through the night and all of yesterday. This as we floundered in the calm, struggling to make two knots, if that. *Jolie Brise* is sailing in 25-knot winds, making 9 knots, and has decreased our lead from 450 nautical miles to 250 miles as of noon today.

During the night the high moved to the southeast, so once again a southwest wind is pushing us, but only just enough to creep along by reaching above the layline for boat speed. This has us sailing to France, not England!

We're seeing spectacular sea life. Zooplankton in this cool water shows up well with a flashlight in the calm and darkness; a special benefit of moving slowly. The bioluminescence is a wonder to us all. Hundreds of translucent, delicate shapes float on a journey with no destination, in contrast to our own goal-obsessed situation. An ounce of speed for ten ounces of sail trim.

Another special benefit of going slowly: the watermaker likes low speed and uprightness so enough water has been made for hair washing with impunity.

Tuesday August 8
1352 GMT (0952 EDT)
Position at 1200 GMT: 48° 53´ N, 12° 34´ W
Making 7 knots on a compass course of 080° magnetic

Tacking downwind in a light south-southwest breeze made for slow progress yesterday afternoon and evening. It finally filled in out of the south and we could lay the finish line, broad reaching at about 7 knots. During our slow escape from the high pressure area in the P.M. hours, our arch-rivals *Jolie Brise* and *Pride of Baltimore II* had enough breeze to make 208 nautical miles and 200 nautical miles, respectively, during the noon-to-noon period. We, on the other hand, logged 150 nautical miles. *Jolie Brise* could ride stronger air as it progresses east and eventually close the lead.

We estimate that *Brilliant* must finish about 15 hours ahead of *Jolie Brise* and within 48 hours after *Pride of Baltimore II* to take first in fleet on corrected time. These three vessels are now first, second and third in the fleet standings, so there is some sense of excitement. We overtook the 300+-foot *Mir* when she was becalmed, but she is now marching up astern at 9 knots with only 20 nautical miles between us. As the gap closes, we'll face similar conditions affecting boat speed. *Pride of Baltimore II* is now ahead of us by 40 nautical miles (about six hours at our present speed) and *Jolie Brise* is about 180 nautical miles astern (about 22 hours at 8.2 knots). The next couple of days will determine the results, and it is not at all out of the question that *Jolie Brise's* better air will give her the lead.

We must not sail into any more holes, but the forecast calls for lighter and more variable air ahead, which we'll encounter before *Jolie Brise*. This doesn't do much for optimism, but we'll take solace in knowing that the bottom of the ocean is lined with optimists, as former *Brilliant* captain Biff Bowker has often said.

Wednesday August 9
1412 GMT (1034 EDT)
Position at 1200 GMT: 49° 24' N, 7°32´ W
Distance to next waypoint: 30 nautical miles
Distance to finish: 200 nautical miles

It's been a busy night of sail changes between the reacher and the #1 – up, down ... up, down – as the apparent wind alternated between just forward of the beam (requiring the #1) and just aft of abeam (requiring the reacher). The reacher is 1.5-ounce cloth and the #1 is 6-ounce so there is a considerable difference in strength as well as shape. Changing sails in these slightly different wind angles is worth about one knot, sometimes amounting to a 10- to 15-percent difference in our speed. This may seem trivial but in fact was crucial to a successful night: we extended our lead over *Jolie Brise* who yesterday had closed the gap to 180 nautical miles. Now, 24 hours later, she's 220 nautical miles astern.

We sailed 202 miles, noon to noon. As long as we can outfoot *Jolie* to the finish or hold our present lead, we think *Brilliant* could take first place in the class on corrected time, and possibly hold on to first in fleet. *Pride of Baltimore* continues to make about 10 knots in this 20-knot southwester so she is lengthening her lead and is now about 82 nautical miles ahead of us.

We have a good following sea, which is corkscrewing us around as we surf down the waves, surging to 11+ knots from an otherwise good average of 9 knots. We're flying everything we have for the broad reach, including pieces of the crew's underwear for the extra one one-thousandth of a knot (and with the hope that it will scare away any evil sea gods). Soon this madness will be over and we can return to a less anxious way with the sea.

The weather forecast suggests a front may go through and bring the southwest wind around to the northwest. That means that all sorts of things can change. There may be pockets of light air with confused seas in the transition period. The lead boats are experiencing different air from the following boats. Everything about this race is still "up in the air."

No sign of mutiny from a still-eager crew.

Thursday August 10
1553 GMT (1153 EDT)
Position at 1200 GMT: 50° 14′ N, 3° 20′ W
Making 7+ knots on a course of 090° magnetic, broad reaching in a light southwesterly wind with a little help from the current

Unless the wind dies tonight – and it may – we expect to arrive at Camper & Nicholsons in Gosport (west of Portsmouth and north of the Isle of Wight) early in the morning of the 11th.

Today's news: we sailed into the English Channel yesterday and made good time broad-reaching through the night, under a damp cold front and with lots of marine traffic working east and west to add a little excitement. We recently tacked to lay the finish line, which is 62 nautical miles ahead in weakening light air. We're worried that we'll get into an all-night drifting match.

Pride of Baltimore II is about 35 nautical miles ahead and also struggling to keep moving. One vessel, *NV Hamburg*, has crossed the line. She's a very well-sailed German sloop but we're not concerned about her early finish; her time correction factor should be generous relative to ours because she's modern. We still stand first in Class CI and in fleet as of noon today, but we won't know if we can hold position until we see if the wind will carry us the next little bit. *Mir*, one of the giant Russian square-riggers, has appeared on the horizon but has been replaced in her Class A lead by another giant, *Kruzenshtern*.

We are now sailing across Lyme Bay and hope to clear Portland Bill before the current turns against us. If we do cross the finish line tonight, we'll probably anchor somewhere in the Solent and arrive at Camper & Nicholsons in the early morning. The crew are in very high spirits. They brought all the brass up to a beautiful shine and gave the decks a good scrub. Showers and dinner ashore are high on tomorrow's priority list. We definitely have race fatigue related to the many sail changes and endless tweaking and careful helm work, as well as the unnatural sleep patterns.

We're fortunate to have had such a smooth crossing and hope that our success thus far in the fleet does justice to the good ship *Brilliant* and her enthusiastic crew.

... later August 10
1830 GMT (1430 EDT)

At this very moment, we're having a rather spectacular and gratifying experience. Under a cloudless sky and with the sun well in the west giving a very special late-day glow, we're reaching beyond Portland Bill and overtaking two large ships: a 182-foot three-masted Dutch schooner, *Eendracht,* and the full-rigged, 312-foot Polish ship, *Dar Mlodziezy.*

Such a clear evening to spend with good company before night, and its cares, falls upon us.

Friday August 11
0550 GMT (0150 EDT)

We crossed the finish line at 0120 GMT this morning (2120 EDT, August 10) and we are now making our way around the northeast corner of the Isle of Wight, soon to be in the Solent. Christine is doing a fine job of navigating in a very busy body of water filled with heavy traffic and a multitude of navigational aids.

We anticipate arriving in Gosport at Camper & Nicholsons about 0900 GMT. We finished a couple of hours after *Pride of Baltimore II*, which fell into light air, and we think we were the third vessel over the finish line, with only *NV Hamburg* ahead of *Pride of Baltimore II.*

The last miles of the race felt like a miracle. Just when we felt sure the air would die and leave us drifting seven nautical miles from the finish, a very strange frontal-type wind shift came in long enough for us to close-reach in a very unfriendly tidal current to the bitter end of the line.

We're confident that we held onto our first place in Class CI and think we'll be first in the fleet on corrected time. *Pride of Baltimore II* will hold first in Class B and fourth in the fleet, we think. *Jolie Brise* was last reported several hundred miles astern of us but nevertheless is holding second in both Class CI and the fleet. *Brilliant's* crew is full of pride.

... later, August 11
1635 GMT
Gosport, England

We were greeted at Camper & Nicholsons' dock by officials of the International Sail Training Association, and friends who have been following *Brilliant's* progress on the Web. By afternoon the ship had a total cleaning and airing with tons of gear spread out on deck and all bodies ashore and in showers. The brass is all shined up. All the customs and immigration details cleared quickly, thanks to the complete list of names, passport numbers, addresses, etc. prepared so thoroughly over months of meticulous follow up phone calls to our participants by Suzanne Reardon of the Education Department at Mystic Seaport.

Brilliant looks like she just left the dock at Mystic Seaport. I thought for sure she'd be showing her seams, especially after the rough conditions in the gale. But no, she shines – and only shows a need for some varnish here and there. Other than the propane solenoid, nothing broke and we arrived with an almost full tank of water, since the watermaker worked fine when we weren't rushing along at hissing speed.

Much of the fleet is now caught in calm air, which we feared would be our fate just short of the finish line. We were so lucky to be able to keep the boat moving in the last of the light air. We heard *Jolie Brise* is still 290 nautical miles from the finish line as of this morning, and she is not alone; only seven of the 34 boats still in the race[7] have finished. How frustrating.

Pride of Baltimore II is docked near us, so we will rendezvous with her crew this evening to celebrate our good luck. Spirits are so high and the sun so bright, we can ask for nothing more.

---

7   Of the forty vessels that originally registered for the race, two did not start and four retired.

Saturday August 12
1048 GMT
Gosport, England

We were able during the race to see the night sky on occasion and talk about celestial navigation. We'll do more on our passages to and from the Canary Islands so that planet locations will become part of our natural awareness. It will fit in well with this group because the book *Longitude* by Dava Sobel has been a popular read on board.

The awards ceremony for the transatlantic race will be held in Amsterdam. We hear there will be 2,000 classic boats attending, in addition to those taking part in the Tall Ships parade. If true, it will be a very busy harbor.

On our way to Holland, we'll make two stops in France at harbors I used to visit when I sailed here in the 1970s. Honfleur and Fecamp are two very small but exceptionally beautiful harbors, and I've been encouraged by the captain of *Esprit*, a 66-foot modern German schooner from Class CII, to take *Brilliant* there. *Esprit's* crew says that *Brilliant* is just the type of boat that would be very welcome in Honfleur. Our crew are very keen to see some of France, so we'll head for Honfleur on Tuesday and after a day or two work our way east to Fecamp.

Today our crew will take the afternoon to see some sights across the river in Portsmouth, such as the HMS *Victory* and HMS *Warrior*, both of which are visible from our spot on Camper & Nicholsons' dock. This is one very busy harbor with lots of big ships coming and going all the time. We enjoyed yesterday evening visiting with the crew of *Pride of Baltimore II* and *Esprit* aboard a lightship that has been converted to a pub. *Pride of Baltimore* is laying alongside the lightship at a marina five minutes' walk from here. We fear for the health of her crew!

Tuesday August 15
1008 GMT
Gosport, England

This afternoon we leave for Honfleur, about 100 nautical

miles south of Portsmouth and just up the River Seine from Le Havre, France. This intimate, fully enclosed harbor is regarded as the most beautiful of Normandy. High water at Honfleur is around 1020 GMT tomorrow and we plan to arrive one hour either side of that, as is recommended. There is a tidal range of about 20 feet and, at low water, only a few feet of depth at Honfleur's entrance off the River Seine.

Locks will take us into the inner harbor, Vieux Bassin, if they have room. We suspect there will be; we've heard that the harbormaster encourages classic yachts to come in because they enhance the harbor's atmosphere. The small, rectangular harbor basin is surrounded by picturesque medieval buildings whose character and architectural integrity have been carefully preserved. We'll probably stay for two days before sailing on to Fecamp, about 30 nautical miles east.

All the crew have enjoyed the fine hospitality at Camper & Nicholsons, with its showers and great convenience to the center of Gosport. All have taken the ferry across the river to Portsmouth to visit HMS *Victory*, HMS *Warrior*, and *Mary Rose*. There is incredible waterfront development going on as Portsmouth and Gosport gear up to become the nautical center of the south coast, if not all of England. They love classic boats here and we have been very welcome.

The International Sail Training Association office is across the street from Camper & Nicholsons, so we can easily keep posted as vessels finish the race. Some have yet to finish but the vast majority are safely over the line. There's no longer much doubt about the results but it may be a day or two before the ISTA office will be able to finalize. Our minds are turning to the adventure of visiting new harbors before the grand finale in Amsterdam.

Wednesday August 16
1612 GMT
Honfleur, France

We safely arrived in Honfleur to a very warm welcome from the harbormaster and others who are delighted to have such a beautiful boat in their showcase. They are providing us with free dockage! We are situated next to the old lock that used to control the inner basin and are in a very visible spot with hundreds of tourists walking by continuously. We have our Mystic Seaport-manufactured portable sign out on the dock and received a bitter complaint from one Frenchman because the sign is in English. "You are in France, no?"

The crew are delighted with this setting and keen to try dinner ashore tonight. Katie has served as our translator. Her nine years of French are at last paying off, even though her classes didn't include "boat speak."

Passage over from England was faster than we anticipated. We arrived off the mouth of the Seine at 0230 GMT and anchored off Deauville-Trouville in a wind-tide-bound, transom-slapping sea for five hours before catching the last of the flood tide on approaching Honfleur, where the lock was opened when we arrived at high water, noon local time.

We'll enjoy this atmosphere and hospitality through tomorrow and then move on to Fecamp, another very small harbor. We hope to find an internet café here so we can send some images of the harbor for quick updates of our experience. The crew is ashore exploring. For many, this is the first time in France! It's so much fun to see so much excitement.

... later, August 16
2049 GMT

I've been thinking back on our race strategy. Our early push east to avoid the heavy weather northeast of the low proved unnecessary. We ended up in a gale equal to the one forecast, but in a different location. Our early easting away from the great-circle route forced us later to run deeper into the high-pressure area than we would have preferred. As a result we didn't have *Pride of Baltimore's* option of reaching up and over the high – unless we turned northwest, away from the finish line and back into the track of those following us from the south. That would be a very uncomfortable move, especially if you're not sure about the location of the center of the high.

Stella Polare, which should have beaten us boat-for-boat by many miles, got so deeply stuck in the high that she never caught us. In fact, she was about 7 days behind us on corrected time. We were lucky to be just a little north of her in the high (by about 100 nautical miles). That gave us just enough light air to move out at about two knots.

We haven't tried to calculate if we could have beaten *Pride of Baltimore II* across the line had we turned northwest to catch better air outside of the high. It would be pure speculation; there are so many variables. I know for sure that we would have done the same as Captain Jan Miles had we been in *Pride's* position further to the west; it would've made no sense to turn east (toward the center of the high) when there was high probability that better air was well to the north.

Some of the faster boats gained a lead on us by going north, but we caught them in the broad-reaching contest of the last few days when *Brilliant* made fantastic time. This crew will never again want to hear the words "cosine," "closing velocity," and "reach for speed." We constantly reached up to the angle that gave us the best closing velocity. I feel sure that made a big difference in those last few days when we strengthened our lead rather than losing it.

At the same time, hindsight is easy. So much depends on "informed speculation" when trying to navigate toward a precise location, for a precise arrival time, or to get the best position with regard to weather systems.

Thursday August 17
Honfleur, France

As of 1200 GMT, all ships in the International Tall Ships Race from Halifax to Isle of Wight have crossed the finish line except *Roald Amundsen*. *Brilliant* is still posted as first in fleet (corrected time) and first in Class CI.

Friday August 18
1850 GMT
In the English Channel, 55 nautical miles from the Dover Strait

We decided to skip Fecamp because of low water depth restrictions in the outer harbor. Pushing on to Holland makes more sense, even though it requires a night passage through

A Message from Skipper George Moffett to Designer Olin Stephens

"You can be just as proud of *Brilliant* as you like," Walter Barnum wrote to boatbuilder Henry Nevins after *Brilliant*'s first Atlantic crossing in 1933. We send you the same message, a little later.

Olin, I know you are not a fan of the schooner rig[8] and I understand why. But there were times when *Brilliant* slid by larger and more modern sloops and ketches in a way that seemed miraculous.

You probably remember Decoursey Fales'[9] comment that a great mystery takes place between the masts of a schooner. There were times in light air when the fisherman, interacting with the top of the main (and perhaps with the help of some upwash from the top of the #1 jib), pulled us along – even when we had no apparent wind at deck level. This may be part of that "mystery" referred to by Fales.

Recent velocity polar plot[10] studies have convinced me that we don't fully understand how schooner rigs work. We certainly don't understand much about the air flow among her interacting sails. But we do know for sure that this rig isn't as fast upwind as those that put more area forward or get more efficiency from spinnakers.

During the race we used a new reacher, which we set flying off the bowsprit and raised or lowered behind the #1 jib. This significantly improved our off-wind performance without the golliwobbler (which we didn't use because of handicapping rules).

On another subject, Rod[11] sailed with us in the last year of his life on an overnight passage from Southport to Mystic. As you might guess, he had suggestions for modifications; one has proven very valuable. We changed the main topping lifts (the old quarter lifts), to a single boom end-to-masthead lift. This made it much easier to handle the main, particularly when reefing.

With the many sail changes of this passage, I often thought of Rod and those couple of days he spent with us.

— Captain George Moffett

8 Stephens designed *Brilliant* with gaff-rigged main and foresail. In 1958, Mystic Seaport changed the main to a marconi rig, to facilitate *Brilliant*'s use as a sail-training vessel. Her foresail remains gaff-rigged.

9 Fales was an award-winning racer and devotee of schooner vessels long after schooners went out of fashion.

10 Velocity polar diagrams show a boat's speed, given a constant wind strength, at various true wind angles. Given this information, a tactician can make more informed decisions.

11 Rod Stephens, Olin's brother and collaborator. Olin specialized in hull design; Rod in rig design.

the Dover Strait. We are motorsailing into a 2-knot current, but we anticipate a fair current through the Strait in the middle of the night. We're still hoping for an arrival in Vlissingen, The Netherlands, late tomorrow.

Sunday August 20
1307 GMT
Vlissingen, The Netherlands

Here we are in Vlissingen, where we'll spend the day before sailing on to Scheveningen, which is about 70 nautical miles from here. From there, it's only 25 nautical miles to IJmuiden. This is a very busy commercial harbor with both mega-shipping and small fishing vessels. The town center and small-merchant activity are only a few minutes' walk from the boat.

We'll depart early in the morning tomorrow to catch the rather strong currents that run along the coast which can have a big effect on progress.

The crew is presently enjoying life ashore. *Pagoria*, a Polish sail-training vessel, lies to the dock only feet ahead of us and Captain Andrzej Szleminski kindly invited me for coffee this morning, where I met many of the ship's crew. Our crew are keen to meet theirs for reasons that I understand are based on international good will – perhaps.

There was an incident on *Pagoria* south of Newfoundland when one of her crew fell 90 feet from the rigging of the foremast and had to be evacuated from the ship. The 21-year-old student is doing well in a hospital in St. John's, Newfoundland. She was lucky. She bounced off multiple parts of the rigging and then fell into a staysail before landing on a cabin top, thus slowing her fall. It seems all she suffered were trauma and hip injuries. She remained conscious upon her arrival on deck and apologized for any inconvenience she might cause. She's a very respected and experienced crew member. Capt. Szleminski is grateful for her good luck and is full of admiration for her spirit and courage.

Kruzenshtern helped with the evacuation, which was done by air from Newfoundland. The entire incident was handled with tremendous professionalism by all, including the Russian ship, which later rejoined the fleet to complete the race.

Right now there are thousands of tourists at the dock who are reading our ship's sign and the banner listing the Web site at Mystic Seaport. Soon there will be a rush of Dutch visitors to Mystic Seaport, since they happily read English.

Monday August 21
0832 GMT
In the North Sea, off the coast of The Netherlands

All's well with *Brilliant's* crew as we enjoy a sunny day sail northeast along the coast between Vlissingen and Scheveningen. We are now 25 nautical miles from Scheveningen, having gotten underway at 0330 GMT (0530 in Amsterdam) to catch the fair tide through the many sand banks that guard the shore. There's no room for navigational laxity in the early part of this passage as we hug the shore with shallows to seaward. It seems the buoy system is very good, since big ships work their way through the shoals without incident.

We're already a bit concerned about the return passage because we'll be going into the prevailing wind. But for now it's an easy slide with the tide and breeze. We're making 8 knots and anticipate arriving in Scheveningen about 1400 GMT, unless the wind weakens and the tide turns.

Tuesday August 22
1245 GMT
Scheveningen, The Netherlands

There are thousands of tourists viewing *Brilliant* along with others in the Tall Ships Fleet here in Scheveningen, which is very near The Hague. The boat looks very good with the varnish, paint, and brass in good shape. Many observers say it is the most beautiful boat in the harbor.

I left a message on voice mail for Paul Cormier, a longtime friend of Mystic Seaport, who teaches at the Law School in Leiden, not too far from here. He kindly stopped by the boat with a bottle of wine and a couple of containers of Brasso, but

I missed his visit.

All is very well with the crew, who are off spending time in The Hague. They love it here because the Dutch are so friendly and happily speak English. The crew is sad to think that tomorrow will be their last sail on this special adventure.

Wednesday August 23
2055 GMT
Dockside, IJmuiden, The Netherlands

Here are some comments from crew about the 2000 International Tall Ships Transatlantic Race and their experiences aboard *Brilliant*:

"A poster of *Brilliant* hangs over my bed. I have occasionally been known to obsessively polish household brass. I wrote my college admission essay about my first trip on *Brilliant*. A race to Bermuda, two Opera House Cups, a summer as cook, and a transatlantic passage later, I'm still learning about the boat, the ocean, myself, and most importantly my shipmates. I have enjoyed a long, salty, and personally transforming passage aboard the finest sailing yacht ever built."

— Katie Oman

"*Brilliant* emblazons itself on your memory in a way that can only partly be described in words. I have stories to tell about crew camaraderie and enduring hardships; I can only hope to recall half of what I've learned from Lee about cooking. The rest are impressions I'll just have to recall without words: the color of Gulf Stream seas, the glow of dawn on salt-encrusted brass and crisp white sails. *Brilliant* is a unique boat. She inspired me to work hard and carry on when I thought I could not. These are things I will carry with me the rest of my life."

— Daniel Parke

"Sailing across the Atlantic Ocean is something I've wanted to do for a long time. The opportunity to do it on a vessel as amazing as *Brilliant* makes me feel exceptionally lucky. Looking back over the last six weeks I see some hardships but mostly good times. I'll remember the days of the gale where we were wet whenever we were on deck and the struggle of trying to clean the head while we were pounding through 10-foot seas in 30 knots of wind. But most of all I will remember coming onto this boat with nine other people I'd never met before and making it through six weeks of sailing without any major incident."

— Myles Thurlow

"These past 6 weeks have enabled me to see and experience things that few people will ever get to experience. I've learned how to tie many different knots, and I can now look in the sky at night and name many stars. Yet if you asked me what the most enjoyable part of the trip was, I'd respond by saying 'the crew.' We worked incredibly well together. If someone needed help or did not understand something, another was there to give a hand and when things needed to be done, they were done fast and well. So out of the sunsets, sunrises, stars, dolphins, whales, sea turtles, huge seas, small seas, little wind, a lot of wind, seasickness, field days, and all the onshore activities, the things that will always remain with me are my memories of this crew and I would be honored to sail with them again."

— Jon Feins

Thursday August 24
0710 GMT
IJmuiden, The Netherlands

We're waiting to enter the locks for the parade up the canal. We're told that two million people are expected to line the banks to view the passing ships. Here we go. It's time to cast off the lines and head for the locks.

... later, August 24
1545 GMT
Amsterdam, The Netherlands

We just arrived safely at the dock in the heart of Amsterdam. All of the crew have gone ashore for showers or to proceed with their own plans. The parade of ships was all that was promised, with staggering numbers of boats and spectators. There are literally millions of people here. Twelve nautical miles of canal banks were filled with observers and enough boats everywhere to walk from one to another. There were many close calls but we managed not to be involved in any collisions. After securing *Brilliant* to the dock, we were almost hit by a spectator boat that lost control. It's a generally overwhelming situation; some might call it madness.

But it feels good to have arrived and to have completed our transatlantic passage.

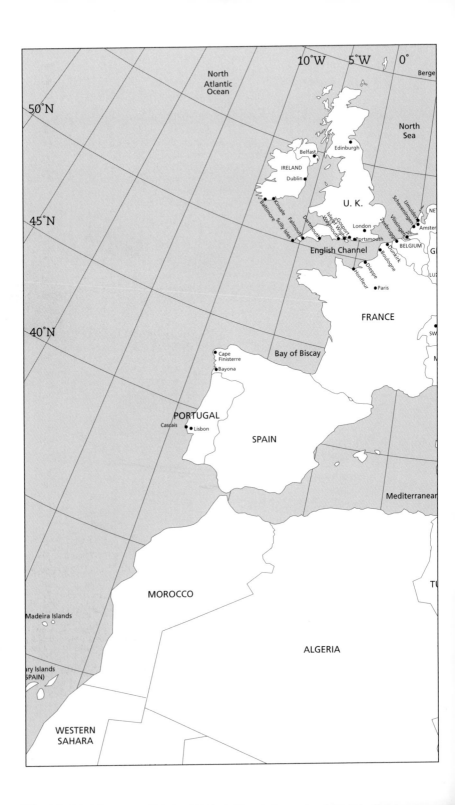

Chapter Two
Lumpy Seas to Lisbon
September 5 - November 18, 2000

*We shift to "cruise," with a change of crew every few weeks ...
discover picturesque ports, powerful currents, extraordinary tides,
and deadly storms ... bask in Romantic lands ... and spend weeks
preparing for the western run.*

Tuesday September 5
1230 GMT
Scheveningen, The Netherlands

Amsterdam has been a wonderland of culture and friend-
ship; we all enjoyed visiting museums and meeting local
people. The crew from the transatlantic race had departed by
August 28th and the new crew started arriving September 2nd.
Brilliant had a few quiet days in between. Our new crew is full
of enthusiasm and willingly rose at 6 A.M. for an early start
down the North Sea Canal to IJmuiden, 12 nautical miles west
of Amsterdam, and then on another 25 nautical miles southwest to Scheveningen.

Our trip through the canal started with considerable
excitement in the lock. Flooding water twisted *Brilliant* around
before we could secure her lines, much to the amusement of
the Dutch canal boatmen. There's an art to going through a
lock; most of it comes down to securing your dockline correct-

47

Crew List
September 3 - September 14
Amsterdam - Gosport, England

Professional Crew

George Moffett, captain
Ledyard, CT

Christine Alberi, mate
Summit, NJ

Mary K. Bercaw Edwards, watch leader
Mystic, CT

Lee Wacker, cook and medical technician
Old Lyme, CT

Cadets

Corey Corbett Brown
Storrs, CT

Sarah S. Fisher
Stonington, CT

Jocelyn McDavit Jensen
Stonington, CT

Florence Renault
Gatteville-Phare, France

Brian Christopher Tabor
Indianapolis, IN

Katrina Anne Yeager
Greenfield, NH

ly the first time. This is a tall order for a new crew on their first day underway. We recovered and were on our way out to sea well before noon.

A fresh northerly wind kicked up a good sea at the harbor mouth, so *Brilliant* plunged down the waves and reached for the sky as we worked our way out through the traffic. It was hard to set sail in these conditions; keeping our feet on the deck required some challenging dance steps. We had beam seas through the entire southwest course toward Scheveningen. Beam seas are very unpleasant for the belly; half of the crew were down with seasickness in quick order.

Luckily the wind backed to the west, giving us a fast reach to Scheveningen.

An early end to the first day of sailing seemed to please everyone. We received a warm reception from the dockmaster, who promised us hot showers. Then we enjoyed dinner, a train ride into The Hague, and a personal tour of the town, thanks to the harbormaster who has taken us under his wing. The Dutch are very friendly people and our visits in Holland could not have been better.

Wednesday September 6
1403 GMT
Zeebrugge, Belgium

This south coast of the North Sea is notorious for its shallows. Only with accurate tide tables and up-to-date charts would one venture through these waters, which can be hazardous – especially at low tide. We worked our way over the sands using excellent charts which we have thanks to the hard work and generosity of Frank Bohlen, who has returned home. We often tacked to slide along one side or the other of unfriendly sand. We sailed over a shoal at high tide, giving us confidence as we approached Zeebrugge.

There's an impressive buoy system here, which enables very large ships to steam at high speeds through narrow channels. They do move right along.

Zeebrugge is a serious shipping port with a small, modern marina tucked away two miles inside the multisectioned harbor. Just outside of the narrow marina entrance, a container ship was being loaded by a contraption of beams and cables high above our heads. With containers stacked so high, it's hard to believe these ships can be stable at sea.

The crew is taking a day in the Flemish town of Brugge, one of Belgium's most beautiful and unspoiled (not bombed) towns. Its 13th-century origins and graceful transition to the 21st century make it a tourist mecca. It's only a 15-minute train ride from Zeebrugge.

Tomorrow we'll push on to France, but haven't decided if we'll continue overnight through the Dover Strait or stop in Dunkirk. The timing of the tide will probably determine this; I don't want to punch through the tide in the Dover Strait and would prefer not to pass through it at night, like we did on our way east.

... later September 6
1840 GMT
Zeebrugge, Belgium

The total distance *Brilliant* sailed from Halifax, Nova Scotia, to Gosport, England, was 2,985 nautical miles; I remember estimating that it would be around 2,800. Since leaving Gosport, we've sailed an additional 573 nautical miles. The total distance sailed this season to date (including trips before leaving New London for Boston), is 4,609 nautical miles.

The Dutch Sparkman & Stephens fan club is extensive. Olin and the yachts he designed are credited as significant factors in revitalizing the country's yacht construction business. A number of Sparkman & Stephens fans, including Harry Heijst, owner of *Winsome*, came to visit *Brilliant* and took me out to dinner.

Thursday September 7
1829 GMT
Dunkirk, France

We arrived safely in Dunkirk this afternoon after a mixture of sailing and motorsailing from Zeebrugge, again zigzagging through shoals. Approaching from the west requires considerable care. Misreading one buoy almost led us to embarrassment.

The wind backed from northwest to southwest today so a fast press to the Strait is impossible. When the tide turns against the wind it kicks up quite a chop, making progress almost impossible on a beat. Furthermore, the forecast includes a possible gale with wind on the nose, so we decided not to push for Dover Strait until tomorrow. We'll decide then if we can press overnight to LeHavre or settle for a long day-sail to Dieppe. Ducking in to Dunkirk was the right call; it's now blowing hard and will build in strength, I think. To the north there are storm warnings, force-10 winds [48 to 55 knots].

The crew remembers Dunkirk from studying European history and they plan to walk the mile into town for some shore life. Now a few words from Mary Kay Bercaw-Edwards:

"I'd forgotten all the stories I'd heard about how tough the North Sea can be. Coming in to Zeebrugge, the rail was underwater much of the day. We were wet, salt-encrusted, and tired, but what fun!

"Brugge is a beautiful medieval town. We climbed the 366 steps to the top of the belfry and saw the red roofs of the town and all the medieval churches. Then we went on a boat ride (we can't stay away from those boats!) on a small, lovely, intimate canal. We got lots of lace and chocolate."

Saturday September 9
1154 GMT
Along the north coast of France, between Boulogne and Dieppe

Yesterday's passage from Dunkirk to Boulogne introduced the new crew to the Dover Strait in a fresh breeze (20 knots) on the nose, with wind against the tide. We had lots of white water on deck on both tacks; we motorsailed on port into the steep seas and sailed on starboard in the much more comfortable beam seas. Currents skewed the waves significantly to favor the starboard tack, which happily worked to our advantage once we reached Cap Gris Nez (Gray Nose), the prominent cape southeast of Dover.

After a long and arduous struggle to reach the Strait

against such strong head winds, we were VERY grateful to have a friendly slide south from Gris Nez to Boulogne. The Boulogne ferry, on overtaking us, slowed for a good look at *Brilliant* before pushing on to arrive about an hour ahead of us. We hadn't intended to stop at Boulogne but exhaustion set in; no one voted for an overnight passage to LeHavre.

Boulogne isn't really set up to host boats of our size, but the harbormaster kindly let us lie alongside a very high (40+ foot) pier. There, we had to contend with a tide range of about 20 feet. There's nothing like climbing down a 40-foot ladder looking at your spreaders within an arm's reach. This arrangement necessitated a night watch to tend dock lines.

Unfortunately, when one line wasn't eased sufficiently in the wake of a big fishing boat, a lifeline padeye fitting pulled right off the rail cap. Damage to the rail cap wasn't significant. Repair will be a matter of extracting and replacing the broken-off 1932 screws; work that cannot be done until we have the right tools and screws. We've relocated the lifeline to a nearby padeye, resolving the safety issue for now.

The mishap was good exposure to the difficulties of docking in such large tidal ranges. It also illustrates why many of the marinas have locked-in basins. The tidal range doubles between Scheveningen and Boulogne. In St. Malo, the tidal range doubles again — to more than 40 feet!

We didn't spend much time ashore. Instead we had a superb dinner from Lee Wacker's portfolio of wonders, combined with some fine wine and fresh bread found within easy walking range of our intimidating dock.

Boulogne is France's busiest fishing port, so wake wash slapped under our stern all through the night, pitching the boat and leaving us unrested.

We rose this morning at 0400 GMT in darkness so we could get underway in relatively calm seas and light air. The seas were initially rough in the blow's aftermath, but soon motor sailing in 7- to 10-knot winds enabled us to lay the line for Dieppe.

With our cell phone we can call harbormasters well-ahead to reserve a spot. Only one place is available in Dieppe for a vessel our size and we just booked it this morning with a late afternoon arrival likely. We're ready for an easy day at sea after days of pounding.

Sunday September 10
Honfleur, France

Everyone enjoyed dinner ashore in Dieppe after showering. Some took time to photograph in the very bright late afternoon light. It was picturesque, indeed: looking down from the high harbor walls into the tidal basin of the modern marina, *Brilliant* virtually glowed with a multitude of small boats in the background, old city buildings framing the scene from above, and a distant church perched on a cliff high above the town.

Who were the engineers who designed this harbor and who were the workers who carved it out and lined it with gigantic blocks of stone? The breakwater alone is an overwhelming structure on a scale difficult to grasp.

Leaving Dieppe, we again were under way by 0400 GMT (0600 local time), which has become our pattern. Days of 60 to 80 nautical miles ending with enough time to walk around necessitate departure at the crack of dawn. We arrived off LeHavre early enough to catch the tide into Honfleur, eight miles up the Seine.

The half tide offered just enough water for a confident ride over the silting bar that lies just before Honfleur's relatively new lock. When I sailed here in the 1970s, the lock was further inside the harbor. The new lock has created a silting problem at the very mouth of the harbor entrance, just as one leaves the main channel of the Seine.

Big ships roar up and down the Seine; traffic is coordinated by a control tower. Passing ships are difficult to see from inside the lock and cross-currents prevent waiting in the exit channel, which is narrow and very short and runs perpendicular to the Seine's own narrow shipping channel. There is little room for error, even for a vessel *Brilliant's* size. When we departed Honfleur a few weeks ago, we didn't know why the control tower was holding us back until we looked through the open lock doors and saw a wall of steel moving by at shocking speed.

We enjoyed Honfleur, a perfect medieval town, which wraps itself so sweetly around the small harbor basin. Earlier today, we sailed along the dramatic high white cliffs that guard the shore in this part of Normandy. Because the light was so good, the entire day was filled with spectacular scenery.

Monday September 11
Honfleur, France

We will clear with the Honfleur harbormaster at 0600 GMT (0800 local time) to catch the lock at 0630 and begin the next-to-last sail with this group. We hope to reach Cherbourg before dark.

Florence, our French crew member, is excited to know that she will be greeted by her parents when we arrive. Her home, next to the lighthouse at the Point of Barfleur, and her place of work, the Maritime Museum of the Island of Tatihou, are nearby. She has helped us communicate with harbormasters and control towers and has provided special historical insights. Now a few words from Florence, who disembarks when we reach Cherbourg:

"I have been so proud and delighted to be aboard *Brilliant*. Every time we entered French harbors, in Honfleur especially, *Brilliant* evoked great admiration from all the people walking by. As a maritime museum staff member, I appreciate *Brilliant* as a jewel on the ocean and also as a wonderful educational tool, perfectly handled under George's guidance. It's amazing to discover in yourself abilities you would never have expected to find.

"I have one question: When do you rig the fishing lines on *Brilliant*? My museum has a fleet of about thirty fishing boats and no yachts.

"Here we are, about 70 nautical miles from my home. Already I know that I will miss my fo'c'sle bunk, Lee's cuisine, polishing brass, standing by the bowsprit for bow watches, etc. It has been a wonderful experience, for which I am so very grateful."

... later, September 11
1200 GMT

We have a fair tide running and are making about 9 knots with 25 nautical miles to go to Barfleur Point Light. Four more hours of fair current should do the trick for a timely arrival, at about 5 P.M. Very light air on the quarter makes motoring necessary. The weather forecast called for wind to go around to the northwest — on the nose. Nevertheless, it's a sunny day and spirits are good.

Lee is very excited about her European land travels, which start next week when Hannah Cunliffe takes over the galley for the next two legs of the voyage.

Now a few words from Sarah Fisher:

"It's amazing to watch seven individuals turn into one well-trained crew in just eight days, very much due to the patience and teaching skill of George and Christine. *Brilliant* is well-received and remarked upon wherever we go. I am astonished at how many people recognize her and know she is from Mystic Seaport! *Brilliant* is a great ambassador."

Perils of Provisioning   September 11, 2000

Hi George,

Thanks for the email and suggestions for shopping, etc. I'm happy to do the provisioning on my own, but would like to talk to Lee [Wacker] about the galley first. It would be best for me to go shopping on Saturday. Stores are open from 10 A.M. to 4 P.M. on Sundays, but it's probably better to get it out of the way on Saturday.

I don't know if you've heard, but we're having a petrol crisis here in England. There are protests all over the country to try and get the prices down. It looks like this might bring things to a bit of a standstill. People are panic-buying petrol. Half of the garages have already run out. We just went to our local garage and they have only 2,000 liters left, of which they had sold 500 by 10 this morning! There may also be power cuts. If people start stocking up on food in case they can't get to the shops, I don't know what the situation will be like by the end of the week. I hope that by then the problem will be resolved. If not, I may not be able to get down to *Brilliant* and could run into difficulties.

Otherwise, all is going well. I look forward to seeing you on Friday. What time is best for Lee? I can meet her in the morning if she wants to get everything sorted early in the day. Hope to hear from you soon. If I don't hear in the next couple of days, I'll call on your cell phone and report on the petrol situation.

—Hannah Cunliffe
[Relief cook, legs three and four: Gosport, England, to Kinsale, Ireland, to Lisbon, Portugal]

Thursday September 14
1533 GMT
Gosport, England

Cherbourg's marina is a vast layout of floating pontoons that ride up and down three-foot-diameter piles and are accessed by seventy-foot-long aluminum ramps, which articulate to meet the tide. Cherbourg's tides range to almost twenty feet.

Mr. and Mrs. Renault, Florence's parents, were waiting at the dock for us when we arrived from Honfleur. They joined us for Lee's fine apple crisp; we'd finished dinner's main course while motoring into the harbor. The day's run had been an eventless motorsail on smooth water and the mood was right for a ride into town with the Renaults, who happily provided a mini tour with a stop at a favored boulangerie for a culinary nightcap of sweet crepes. Many days of rising at 6 A.M. and turning in after 10 P.M. took their toll: all were in their bunks before the wee hours.

Another early start Tuesday morning for our return to Gosport, England, received groans of protest. We fueled up in France (at $3 a gallon) because we'd heard about the fuel strike in England. We weren't sure if it was wise to arrive there with a light tank. It turns out that there is diesel but not gas (petrol) here at Camper & Nicholsons, where we're now docked comfortably.

We're next to the construction and launching area of this yard, which produced the best of British boats during the same decades that Herreshoff and Nevins were producing the best in the U.S. This is where *Altair*, a Fife schooner the size of Mystic Seaport's *L.A. Dunton*, is maintained at a level that makes *Brilliant* look neglected.

Among the vessels being serviced here is a new 73-foot sloop that will be carried on the deck of her mother ship — an American-owned, 350-foot motor yacht — along with a 70-foot powerboat that serves as tender. It's not clear to us why a 350-foot ship needs a 73-foot sloop, unless it's recreation for the more than 30 crew. Suddenly *Brilliant's* operations budget seems reasonable. I've been counting the cost of about 150 gallons of diesel and 60 pounds of propane used since we left the U.S.

We arrived here with a virtually full tank of diesel because a fair wind of 15 to 20 knots gave us a fast passage from France to England in 10 hours flat, harbor to harbor. Christine [Alberi, *Brilliant's* mate] navigated and took full command all the way across the Channel and into the busy waters of the Solent, all smoothly executed.

This morning we thoroughly cleaned the ship before the

Crew List
September 17 - September 27
Gosport, England - Kinsale, Ireland

Professional Crew

George Moffett, captain
Ledyard, CT

Christine Alberi, mate
Summit, NJ

Tom Cunliffe, watch leader
Salisbury, UK

Hannah Cunliffe, cook
Salisbury, UK

Cadets

Theo Nicholas Botha
Exeter, Devon, UK

Shannon Parke Colgary
Mystic, CT

Earl David Hergert
Somerville, NJ

Tober Jackson Schorr
Bellingham, WA

Neil Simms
Kirdford, West Sussex, England

Kelly Marie Smit
Phoenix, MD

crew took the ferry across the harbor to visit the HMS *Victory* and HMS *Warrior* at the Royal Naval Museum and Dockyard in Portsmouth.

Sunday September 17
Gosport, England

The new crew joined us today, trickling in throughout the afternoon. Some went to visit the Naval Museum; others relaxed in Gosport before dinner. The evening ended with safety lectures and drills in the darkness. A few of us enjoyed a nightcap at the marina pub, which is full of Camper & Nicholsons photos of famous yachts built or serviced at the yard. Hannah Cunliffe's first dinner cooked aboard *Brilliant* received "oohs" and "aahs" — a measure of complete success.

Monday September 18
Cowes, Isle of Wight, England

More safety drills this morning led to preparations for the sail across the Solent to Cowes. It's not a great distance, but there is a lot of traffic and some places where one could go aground. Tom Cunliffe knows these waters well and served as our navigator, keeping stress to a minimum. Sailing in heavy rain and 22- to 27-knot winds (with gusts) was no warm welcome, but it did wake us up to the challenge of sailing in these waters. The warm welcome came later in the evening.

A double-reefed main with fore and forestaysail gave us 8 knots on the wind and multiple tacks took us into Cowes early in the afternoon. A well-protected spot at the Yacht Haven, made possible by friends of *Brilliant* from the Island Sailing Club, gave us security for the evening. The Club also held a wonderful party for us, with more than 30 guests, who visited *Brilliant* at the dock before a reception and dinner, where spirited conversation was spiked with Pimms aplenty and wine generously poured.

A Warm Wight Reception

Stan Malone, at the request of Neil Simms, organized a wonderful reception at the Island Sailing Club. Our friends at the Club put tremendous thought into their reception and dinner party welcoming *Brilliant* to the Isle of Wight. The crew was assigned to tables by twos, so we were widely represented. The written dinner program included a 1933 article from *Yachting World*, which welcomed *Brilliant* to Solent waters for the Royal Ocean Racing Club's Fastnet Race. The Mayor of Cowes, John Leigh, a keen supporter of Isle of Wight sailing programs, joined us at Commodore John Dudley's table with John Power, Chairman of Cowes Yachting and a generous supporter of *Brilliant's* reception.

Fiona Brothers, who is famous for her success at world-class motorboat racing, and Rosemary Joy, a leader in the development of the Classic Boat Museum near Cowes, were key facilitators for the event. We heard speeches from Commodore Dudley, John Power, Andy Cassell (an Olympic racer and partner in the Ratsey and Lapthorn firm of sailmakers) and from photographer Keith Beken, from the famous Beken of Cowes studio.

Keith presented us with a Beken photo of *Brilliant* taken at the start of the 1933 Fastnet Race and a copy of *The Beken Album*, a new book of photos with text by William Collier. Andy gave *Brilliant* a copy of *Classic Sails, The Ratsey and Lapthorn Story*, also written by William Collier. Some may remember that Collier spoke at a Mystic Seaport Yachting History Symposium a few years ago.

The next day Rosemary Joy took us by bus to the town of Newport for a visit to the Classic Boat Museum, an absolute must for small craft enthusiasts seeking the best of England's vacation spots. Maurice Wilmot and Kim Lyall gave us a personal tour of the collection which included two perfectly restored Chris Crafts. The boats in this collection are fully operational and therefore do not seem like static artifacts, the way vessels do when they haven't seen water for years.

We were sincerely pleased and grateful for the warm hospitality.

— Captain George Moffett

Wednesday September 20
Weymouth, England

Tuesday's tide-sensitive departure from Cowes, at noon, required sailing out of the harbor with the wind just right for mild drama. An Island Sailing Club member asked that we set sail early for photo opportunities. We managed to be under full sail, including the fisherman, as we passed the Club and fired a salute with the 10-gauge cannon that Rudie Schaefer[1] gave us years ago. It also seemed appropriate to salute the Royal Yacht Squadron. If a strong, echoing report is any indication, we were probably heard! It was a poignant conclusion to a grand visit.

The current would be against us for two hours on our approach to the Needles at the west end of the Solent. But Tom's local knowledge (he's the editor of the *Shell Channel Pilot*, a reference book for navigating the English Channel) led us to hug the south shore where the current was fair. We reached the narrows as the tidal flow reversed and were carried all the way to Weymouth, arriving at dusk.

One lives by the tidal currents in these waters, so we planned to depart from Weymouth Wednesday morning at 0500 GMT (0600 local time). We hoped this would give us a fair run for the eight miles from Weymouth and enable us to catch the last of the fair current around the notoriously turbulent Portland Bill, where a foul tidal current would be unbearable. After rounding this point, the remaining 40 nautical miles to Dartmouth would be easy; we'd arrive with time to spend ashore.

So we hoped. Upon rising at 0530, we were greeted by heavy rain and a BBC weather forecast that warned of possible strong headwinds. We elected to spend a day in Weymouth — a popular choice, even though the weather report was wrong. The front came and went early, leaving a clear day with light winds.

We took long walks along Weymouth's sandy shore and wandered through town, viewing its regency architecture

---

1   Former President and Chairman of the Board of Trustees for Mystic Seaport. The Schaefer family have long been benefactors of the Museum.

from the George III era. Tom Cunliffe and Neil Simms provided historical details. Hannah produced a very fine dinner with yet another great pudding, which concluded the day for all but those whose sense of tradition obliged a run to the pub.

Friday September 22
Off the southwest coast of England, near Falmouth

Ironically, weather conditions became even worse after our lay day in Weymouth. On the sail to Dartmouth, gale-force winds gusted to 40 knots and gave us a challenging, hold-on-for-your-life ride with most of the crew diving for seasickness pills. We had lots of white water on deck. Everyone was soaked and sometimes submerged. Tom Cunliffe summed it up: "This boat is rather wet!"

Certainly, none of us will ever forget this passage. Happily, it was over early enough to enjoy the beautiful town of Dartmouth. It is nestled in the deep valley of the River Dart and offers one of the more spectacular approaches among many on the West Country coast. Dartmouth was bathed in sunlight as we bent around Mew Stone to catch sight of a hidden harbor with a narrow entrance between castles and vertical rock. This West Country coast is dominated by tall cliffs with a mixture of jagged gray or brown rock and muted shades of green, often capped with a patchwork of rich green farmland in small irregular fields, bordered here and there with stone fences.

Driven as always by the need to catch the tide, we left early today, at 0630 (0530 GMT). Now, eight hours later, we are only one hour from arrival in Falmouth. We very nicely caught the "tidal gate" around the headland just south of Dartmouth (Prawle Point), and hours later came close enough for a good look at Eddystone Light, about which chanteymen have sung so often. Tom, a great one for a song, gave us his rendition as the massive column diminished off our stern. We've had a fast motorsail today with the wind southwest at 7 to 10 knots; now it's south at 7 to 10 and sometimes 11 to 16 knots.

We expect the wind will be southeast tomorrow, after a front passes tonight (we hope). Another early departure will get us around Land's End with the tide. But first we'll have some fun in Falmouth this afternoon and tonight.

Now some words from crew member, Earl Hergert:

"While polishing brass today, I had time to ponder ... why are we out in the middle of the sea? Certainly *Brilliant* herself is reason enough — such a wonderful vessel! The beauty of the sea and English countryside is another good reason. But for me, the crew is the best part of sailing. Everyone works together for the mutual benefit and survival of everyone else. It is utopian and primeval at the same time. The only thing missing is my wife!"

Saturday September 23
1622 GMT
Atlantic Ocean, 20 nautical miles northwest of the Isles of Scilly;
113 nautical miles from Kinsale, Ireland
Making 9 knots of boat speed; 20 knots of wind on the ship's quarter

At 0545 GMT, we cast off the lines in Falmouth to catch the tide around Land's End on our way to Ireland. The weather looks more unstable with this morning's report; there may be a northwester later in the day. If so, it'll be right on the nose. It was extremely difficult to rise this morning because it was the third morning in a row that we woke in darkness to beat the tide. Furthermore, some found Falmouth's popular pub, The Chain Locker, an irresistible temptation last night and stayed perhaps one pint too long.

Nevertheless, we were underway as planned and rounded the Lizard[2] exactly as intended, to catch the fair tide to Land's End by noon. Thus we enjoyed the last of the westing wind and the first of the northing as we laid a course north of the Isles of Scilly. A force five southeast wind kicked up some seas that were awkward on a broad reach, but we've managed to maintain a steady eight knots, now under conservative canvas: three lower sails and a reef in the main.

With the tide sweeping us north of our course, west was the best we could lay, given the southeast breeze. We found ourselves heading for the reef known as Seven Stones, so we

---

2 England's southernmost point.

had to jibe at the last minute to avoid disaster. An unmanned lightship marks this reef, which lies near the inner shipping lanes that run between Land's End and the Isles of Scilly.

We are making such good time that we expect to arrive in Kinsale early tomorrow morning. The southeast wind has veered to the south, enabling us to steer a course of 305° magnetic. We need 327° to lay Kinsale.

I emailed our contact in Kinsale to see if it would be okay to stay at the Yacht Club dock. We've hoped for that arrangement since I visited Kinsale two years ago to explore this trip's possibilities. The crew are eager to enjoy the friendliness of the Irish; this harbor will be the right place to start.

Sunday September 24
0259 GMT
41 nautical miles from Kinsale, Ireland

It's the black of night, the Moon is rising and Orion is bright and well up in the south. What a night! All on watch are feeling high because the wind is driving us along at 8 knots. It's coming out of the west with enough south in it for a nice close reach on a heading of 325° magnetic. We anticipate reaching Kinsale well before noon. Ahead, some gas wells loom on the horizon but otherwise nature is a powerful presence, complete with dolphins that have been diving off the bow for hours.

Sunday October 1
1446 GMT
Kinsale, Ireland

After a week in Ireland, *Brilliant* has had a change of crew and we're finalizing our plans to depart for France and points beyond. We've had long discussions about the weather this morning, with the aid of multiple weather maps and the sage advice of the crew of *Asgard II*, the Irish sail-training ship, which is here in Kinsale with us. It looks like a large high-pressure system is moving east toward the Bay of Biscay; before that, a low could give us winds of 20 to 30 knots on the nose as we move off the west coast of France. That's not what we want. Delaying our departure until Tuesday may give us fair winds all the way into Biscay — if we don't stop in France.

The very experienced Irish crew of *Asgard II* say we'd be unwise to go east into France with these weather patterns, since we'd risk facing a long beat into the wind upon leaving Douarnenez. So, unfortunately I feel we must skip our visit to that city. Florence Renault, who sailed with us in France a few weeks ago, put great effort into setting up a rendezvous in Douarnenez, so I make this decision with great regret.

... later October 1
2116 GMT
Kinsale, Ireland

Our departure date and time are still up in the air. The weather looks unfriendly for anyone heading south. I've been pulling weather maps from our fax this afternoon and evening and have a very clear set of prognostic maps out to 24, 48, and 72 hours. These are coming from the internet via Mick Loughnane of Sail Ireland, and from *Asgard II*, which is still laying to our stern.

We won't stop in Douarnenez because of the recent gales and storms and the forecast for 30-knot winds out of the south-southwest on October 3rd. Fair winds tomorrow tempt me to go for it, but I fear we'd sail about 100 nautical miles south only to have the wind back and blow 34 to 40 knots long enough to exhaust our crew, with miles yet to reach port.

The 72-hour forecast offers hope that a big high-pressure center currently west of Biscay may come in with fair winds on October 4th. But we could miss that window if we don't leave Kinsale tomorrow and slog through heavy weather on the 3rd. If the 48-hour forecast is right, we won't be able to leave on the 3rd because it'll be blowing 30 knots on the nose all the way to Biscay.

Gads, what a mess ... the weather summary shows three gales moving on Ireland at this time! Taking Douarnenez out of the schedule saves two days or more; that takes pressure off the schedule, but means a 600 mile slog to Spain.

I knew this leg would be difficult, but didn't imagine it

Crew List
October 1 - October 11
Kinsale, Ireland - Lisbon, Portugal

Professional Crew

George Moffett, captain
Ledyard, CT

Christine Alberi, mate
Summit, NJ

Sally McGee, watch leader
Alexandria, VA

Hannah Cunliffe, cook
Salisbury, UK

Cadets

Kristene Genevieve C. Boucher
Beaver Dam, WI

Eric Chanu
St. Malo, France

Shannon Parke Colgary
Mystic, CT

Margaret Anne Gryn
Doylestown, PA

Lucas Aldo Knuttel
Guilford, CT

Kate M. Simmons
Washington, DC

would be this agonizing before we even cast off the lines! It is blowing like fury right now and has been most of the day, as this deep low slides over us. This weather is truly classic stuff, right out of the textbook. It would be a big mistake to take this new crew straight into heavy seas, so I think we'll do some day sailing tomorrow to warm up and clear the blood. Speaking of which, the entire crew are down at the Mad Monk to hear some traditional Irish music, while I'm hanging here to review the options and sweat the decision, as a captain should.

Monday October 2
1952 GMT
Kinsale, Ireland

We just enjoyed a wonderful dinner cooked by Hannah, which lifted our spirits, despite the rain falling yet again, as a front moves through ahead of the next low. We day-sailed today after a morning of instruction from Christine on safety, handling lines, bending on sails, taking in reefs on the main, and using the winches.

We sailed with a double-reefed main, heavy-weather jib, forestaysail, and fore, all moving us along nicely at nine knots in a force-6 wind. Solid seas reminded us of the strong low that blasted through yesterday, and the sail out to and beyond Old Head gave everyone a feel for the exposed ocean waves. As the locals would put it, we sailed in the lee of Bermuda! All went well with a man overboard drill under sail. We feel more confident now. Everyone understands the wisdom of waiting to see what will come of the large low moving in from the southwest [remnants of Hurricane Isaac], which is anticipated to carry force-10 winds on its west side. If it weakens or is forced north by the high off Biscay, we may be able to move out tomorrow. However, local wisdom still recommends that we remain here until Thursday when the seas will have eased.

If we stay in Kinsale tomorrow, we'll do another day sail to firm up our skills and ability to deal with heavy weather. Sailing along the shore today gave the new crew a chance to appreciate the beauty of the Irish coast and the spectacular entrance to Kinsale, guarded by Charles Fort. All of this made our stay seem well worth the delay. We gave some of the locals a sight by sailing out of, and back into, the inner harbor. The crew is now headed ashore for nightlife with the Irish.

Wednesday October 4
1118 GMT
Kinsale, Ireland

We plan to depart at 1200 GMT today even though there is considerable wind and a good sea running. We want to reach the high to the south and we must get out of here before the next strong low arrives. We'll have to beat into a 20-knot southwester for awhile, but later it will ease, shift to the northwest, and go light, so we may be motoring.

The harbormaster has been very generous with his advice about the weather and has given me regular printouts from the Web, mostly NOAA information. Mick Loughnane, the *Asgard II* crew, and Billy the marina manager for the Kinsale Yacht Club have also been very helpful in many ways. Kinsale has been a wonderfully friendly place to visit; our ten days here could not have been better, even with the high winds and heavy rain. We'll keep you posted on our progress since there is probably concern from all with this weather situation.

I spoke with the captain of *Palawan* [an S&S design built for IBM Chairman Thomas J. Watson and now owned by Mystic Seaport Trustee, Joe Hoopes] today by phone while in the harbormaster's office. They'll probably arrive here tomorrow, so we'll just miss seeing them.

... later October 4
1422 GMT
Two hours out of Kinsale, making about 8 knots

We are in very rough seas and having to sail close-hauled to make 160 degrees. We're hoping the wind will go more west when this front passes. Will we be happy when we find ourselves further south! The deck is covered with white water; waves occasionally break over us. We're diving off some waves and slamming into others. We're rigged with double-reefed main, fore, forestaysail, and no jib.

Thursday October 5
0416 GMT
Current position: 49° 50' N, 8 ° 30' W
Speed over the ground: 9.5 knots

We just sailed by a cable-laying ship. The wind is more on the beam now, blowing a good 25 knots. Our speed is steady.

... later October 5
1356 GMT
Position at 1200 GMT:48° 50' N, 8° 52´ W
Making 8.5 knots on a course of 195 degrees magnetic

Sextant observations at 1230 GMT, taken at the peak of 10-foot swells: height of eye above the water was 4 feet. Two sights were taken of the sun's lower limb: 36° 02.3´ with an index correction of +1.0 minutes and 36° 03.0´ with an index correction of zero minutes. Position by GPS at the time: 48° 45´ N, 8° 54´ W

We're experiencing long swells with gentle wavelets and a beam wind of about force 4. Perfect! I hope it holds, but anticipate the high-pressure system will necessitate motoring soon. We can feel the wind easing as the barometer rises rapidly, now reading 30.25 inches compared with 28.95 inches at one point in Kinsale when the low pressure system passed by us.

We're flying our reaching sails to keep *Brilliant* moving. Sun, warmth, and the boat's kindly motion have us all in good spirits. We had one little scare this noon when the engine wouldn't start, but concluded that the big seas had run some water into the exhaust pipe and over-filled the silencer. We drained the water and she started like a charm. Now a few words from watch leader Sally McGee:

"Many of us have anticipated and perhaps romanticized the notion of a passage from Ireland to Lisbon, but there's nothing like yesterday's choppy, confused sea and the remnants of a significant low-pressure system to remind you who's in charge: "Mom" Nature, always. This morning, with the incoming high, we have a long gentle swell and a 10- to 12-knot breeze that we hope will persist through the next 48 hours and carry us to Finisterre. For now, pilot whales, dolphins, petrels, and other birds accompany us as we approach the edge of the continental shelf. On a day like this there's nowhere else we'd rather be!"

Friday October 6
0757 GMT
Current position: 46° 35´ N, 9° 23´ W
Light air from the east
Motoring at 6.5 knots in smooth seas with 8- to 9-foot swells

There appears to be a front to the west and heavy cloud cover is coming in. The area around Spain's Cape Finisterre has its own weather system, often completely different from everything else surrounding it, so we really cannot be very precise on our estimated time of arrival. My revised ETA for Bayona, Spain, is early Sunday October 8, assuming we maintain our speed for the duration of the trip. The Inmarsat shipping forecast indicates winds of force 6 to 7 [22 to 27 knots / 32 to 38 knots] with possible force 8 [34 to 40 knots] in the Cape area today, but we hope that will pass by the time we arrive there. Otherwise, it confirms NOAA's weather map surface analysis and the 72-hour forecast map that I got before leaving Kinsale. We are very lucky to have had such a gentle crossing of the Bay of Biscay — so far.

We topped off with fuel in Kinsale, anticipating that we'd be motoring through this high. For now, I'm confident that we'll have no trouble reaching Bayona by Sunday. Now a few words from Margie Gryn:

"Conditions here are much more calm than I had expected (knock on wood); being on watch starts to feel like driving across Nebraska. Yesterday we had a fair number of dolphin sightings and this morning we had a beautiful sunrise. Everyone seems to be in good spirits. We're beginning to see evidence of cabin fever, however, as "punchiness" begins to run rampant. I think we're all finally settled into the rocking of the boat and the watch-dictated sleeping times. Things are running smoothly and everyone is enjoying themselves. I must say though, I'm looking forward to seeing land again."

... later October 6
1919 GMT
Position at 1200 GMT: 46° 8´ N, 9° 31´ W
Current position: 45° 17´ N, 9° 40´ W
Making 6 to 7 knots under sail, on a course of 190 degrees magnetic.
Approximately 138 nautical miles north of Cape Finisterre.

No noon sight taken. (Blame "brain failure" and being absorbed with a shaft bearing project.)

Saturday October 7
0704 GMT
Current position: 43° 44´ N, 9° 40´ W, about 30 nautical miles north of Finisterre, Spain
Making 8 to 9 knots

Some helpful air has filled in out of the northeast and we've shortened sail again. We're now ahead of our revised ETA; we may make it to Bayona by late this evening. We have motored only about 15 hours because the easterly winds came in earlier than the forecast had indicated.

Over the next few hours we'll be cutting across the heavy shipping traffic, electing to do it north rather than south of the restricted shipping lanes around Cabo Finisterre. To that end, we altered course to the east, 175 degrees magnetic. Daylight has just welcomed us to a beautiful morning of lively seas and 20 knots of fresh Biscay breeze.

... later October 7
1254 GMT

Cabo Finisterre is abeam, three miles off. Distance to Bayona is 53 nautical miles with an ETA of 2000 GMT. Dozens of dolphins are around us. Mountainous cliffs are nearby. Cameras are clicking. The crew is overwhelmed.

... later October 7
2152 GMT

We arrived at Bayona, Spain, 52 minutes ago, at 2100 GMT.

Monday October 9
1131 GMT
Along the coast of Portugal, 150 nautical miles north of Cabo Carvoeiro

We're under way again, heading toward Lisbon on a course of 190 degrees magnetic so as to clear Cabo Carvoeiro. We're very grateful to have crossed Biscay when we did, as there are now force-9 and possible 10 [48 to 55 knots] storm warnings for the area we just sailed through three days ago.

We were very lucky to have had the weather-window we enjoyed after the initial slog through the Celtic Sea. I didn't report this earlier, but we were falling off the back side of those post-gale steep waves south of Ireland and slamming very hard — the hardest I've ever experienced. But *Brilliant's* seams are not showing, even after all that pounding. It's a tribute to her builders that she can take this stuff so well in her maturity and look like she just came out of the yard.

Three days from Ireland to Bayona is quite respectable. Our night arrival in Bayona was without mishap, although the range lights for the approach through the rocks were missing. With lighted buoys and a clear, moonlit night, the approach was low-stress. Jagged, dramatic mountains run right down to the shore with villages nestled in every possible gap, a sight that kept us in awe until sunset.

As we worked our way into the harbor, we were greeted at 2200 local time (2000 GMT) by an elderly gentleman in a small boat. He guided us to our dock spot, which required a stern-to Mediterranean-style approach. We set our anchor before realizing he had bow lines ready, distressing the man in the boat just a bit. We communicated with sign language and dramatic shrugs to indicate the miserable hopelessness of retrieving the anchor at such a late hour.

Bayona's nightlife was in full swing, so the crew were allowed to rush ashore without doing the usual tasks of hos-

ing down and cleaning the boat. It was clearly the right decision: the evacuation of *Brilliant* took mere seconds with our
desperadoes virtually sprinting into the village. Some didn't
return until 3 A.M. Alone, the wholesome and mellow-spirited
captain stayed with the ship to enjoy a full night's rest, and
particularly enjoyed waking the crew for their morning brass-
polishing chores. Curiously enough, the call was not appreciated, but the ship's work was done in time for all to go ashore
again. Bayona called, in the full brightness of a warm sunny
day.

The Monte Real Club de Yates nestles shoreside in a
Disneyesque castle and offers a fine view of the harbor.
Shower and other facilities could not be more elegant. One vis-
itor took great interest in *Brilliant*: Alfredo Lagos, who is a Port
Officer of the Royal Cruising Club and Ocean Cruising Club,
owns a boatyard in Vigo, Astilleros Lagos, and has many
friends in the Cruising Club of America.

Now a few words from Shannon who, it seems, has found
neither Ireland nor Spain a disappointment:

"I've been away from home for nearly a month now, and
just when I think that I couldn't possibly have a more amazing
time, it gets even better. The unbelievable landscapes, the fabulous people — what more could a girl ask for? Bayona is
breathtaking in more ways than one! The mountains are skirt-
ed with white sandy beaches, the Spanish barmen wait to
sweep you off your feet with Latin dancing. My head is still
spinning from last night's salsa session.

"By day, Bayona is a busy tourist town with more shops
and cafes than I can begin to count. By night, the Spanish
show their spirit in the discotecas. Even on Saturday night,
with three days worth of boat grime on us and sleep in our
eyes, we had the time of our lives. England ... Ireland ... Spain
... and now onto Portugal. What is in store, no one knows, but
there's no doubt that the next five days will be truly unforget-
table."

Tuesday October 10
0644 GMT
Current position: 39° 20´ N, 9° 28´ W
Making 7.4 knots on a course of 195 degrees magnetic

We're off Cabo Carvoeiro with about 40 nautical miles to go for Cabo Raso, which is where we turn left to enter Lisbon. We anticipate arriving in Lisbon about 1400 GMT, which is 1500 local, we think.

... later October 10
1211 GMT
Position at 1200 GMT: 38° 45´ N, 9° 32´ W

We are motoring around Cabo Raso, a very impressive mountainous rise dwarfing all human activity. We are a mere speck. Arrival at APORVELA, Portugal's sail training association, is revised to 1630 GMT. All aboard are healthy and full of anticipation as we approach yet another scenic wonder. What an earth we have!

... later October 10
2004 GMT

We went up the river to dock at APORVELA, only to find that they had made a mistake with both us and *Pride of Baltimore II*: they don't have the depth of water to handle either of us. Funny, because I included all that information in my letters a year or more ago. In any case, we're next to *Pride* at a marina called Doco de Alcantara, a very large marina with minimal facilities and no feeling of security, located near a large suspension bridge that spans the Rio Tejo, which Lisbon faces. I had to walk two miles to clear customs, just to give you an idea how remote this marina is.

Pride of Baltimore II was in Baltimore, Ireland, when we were in Kinsale. She took a real beating in the heavy weather with winds that exceeded 60 knots. It was all her crew could manage to keep resetting her anchors. She finally escaped the harbor the same day we did, only to take the same hammering. It's my understanding that she left later in the day and may have benefited from the wind going around to the north, whereas we beat for hours into a southwester. In any case, here we lie on opposite sides of the same pontoon dock. How strange.

I'm seriously considering moving the boat to Cascais, on the outskirts of Lisbon. It's 15 miles down the river from here, closer to Madeira and has a better facility. *Geronimo*, a yacht from St. Georges (a private school in Newport, RI) was in Bayona when we arrived; her skipper recommended Cascais. We passed it several hours before we arrived here, and I had wished we'd arranged to be there. I'm 90 percent sure we'll want the new crew to meet us there. I'm pretty sure Suzanne Reardon [of the Education Department at Mystic Seaport] can reach all those who are joining us and let them know where we'll be.

Friday October 20
Cascais, Portugal

The Cascais Marina suffers a tremendous surge, which has given us serious problems keeping the boat safe at its location by the dock. Dr. Manuel Leitao, a Portuguese friend of Olin Stephens who visited us yesterday, said there has been much discussion about the notorious surge. The breakwater constructed for the marina isn't adequate to deal with the very large seas and swells typical on this coast.

Two nights ago I was up all night tending lines and fending off the dock. The next morning the marina launch ran a line out to a piling to help pull us off the dock. Things are better now, but last night Dan Bregman and I still had to double up lines and replace a 3/4-inch nylon line that had chafed through on the dock cleat!

We have chafing protection gear all over the boat, but I'd say we've done more damage to dock lines and sheets (serving as dockline backups) than in the past 20 years combined. That's how bad it is.

If they build an additional breakwater to take the reflected swells that come from the neighboring beach, perhaps it will help. But it seems to have been a mistake to build a marina in such an exposed area. The investors who started all this have run out of money, so there are unfinished aspects all around; essential features like showers and heads are poorly maintained.

Dan Bregman arrived yesterday afternoon and Rich King came today. Lee Wacker rejoined us a couple of days ago. Dan had extra excitement when his bag went missing, but the airline found it and delivered it to the marina. Lee and Christine went to Sintra yesterday and returned this afternoon. This gave Christine a chance to get off the boat for a while.

Sintra is a small town in the hills just north of Cascais and was a vacation spot for the royal family until the revolution in 1910. It remains a popular tourist destination and vacation spot for the rich. There are large houses scattered through the hills that surround Sintra. Both Cascais and adjacent Estoril benefit from the same concentration of wealth. But we hear that the most spectacular vacation spots are on Portugal's south coast, with Sagres, west of Lagos, being the most beautiful. Lee Wacker visited Sagres and raved about its dramatic setting on giant cliffs. When Hannah Cunliffe left us in Lisbon with her friend Nicola, their first destination was Sagres. It's hard to believe we'll soon be under way for Madeira.

... later October 20
2059 GMT

We're enjoying a partly clear sky and a much calmer marina after a strong northerly calmed the seas that had driven the surge. It was a cool evening on deck for a chat with new arrivals. An extremely bright planet was setting in the west at sunset — so bright we couldn't believe it was a planet. As we watched its steady decline during nightfall, we started to acknowledge that it wasn't a plane with bright landing lights.

I concluded from the Celesticomp donated by Bill Croughwell, a longtime friend of Mystic Seaport, that the object had to be Venus; none of the other planets are visible at sunset where we are. Venus was so bright it looked like you could reach out and grab it.

We'll start watching the heavens so we know what to "shoot" at sunset and sunrise. We now have four sextants aboard, counting Rich King's new gift,[3] so we'll probably have mega celestial work going on throughout the crossing, and some prepping on the way to the Canaries. We'll try to make it a feature of this passage.

The passage west is promising to be far more relaxed than the race across proved to be. Things feel so mellow now, which gives me an idea just how stressed I was for the first couple of legs of this program. I'm sure that others felt the stress too.

... still later October 20
2211 GMT

We just had a good look at what we conclude is Jupiter rising. It was very bright and clear, but not nearly as bright as Venus. We think we see Saturn to the right and above Jupiter, not nearly as bright.

Wednesday October 25
1351 GMT (0951 EDT)
Position at 1200 GMT: 33° 51′ N, 15° 20′ W
Making 9 knots on a course of 230 degrees magnetic
Wind is from the north at force 5

We anticipate arriving in Madeira about 2 A.M., having covered more than 400 nautical miles in 48 hours. All are recovering from seasickness; most are starting to eat again. It couldn't be better sailing, except for an overcast sky.

... later October 25
2004 GMT

Land ho! The northeastern-most island of the Madeira group became visible through a haze at about 1730 GMT, with its volcanic spire rising 515 meters. It gave us an idea how the

---

3 A sextant from his friends aboard *Harvey Gamage* and in the Williams College-Mystic Seaport Maritime Studies Program.

Crew List
October 22 - November 1
Cascais, Portugal - Tenerife, Canary Islands, Spain

Professional Crew

George Moffett, captain
Ledyard, CT

Christine Alberi, mate
Summit, NJ

Rich King, watch leader
Mystic, CT

Lee Wacker, cook and medical technician
Old Lyme, CT

Cadets

Daniel Evan Bregman
Queens, NY

Donald Ferguson Hambidge
Mystic, CT

Holly Alexa Hawkins
Stonington, CT

Donna Kelly
Noank, CT

John Merrill, Jr.
Waterford, CT

Brittan Anne Weinzierl
U.S. Army, based in Germany

Portuguese explorer Zarco must have felt upon finding this shelter (Porto Santo) during a gale back in 1418. This is where Columbus walked the beaches with his bride, about fifty years after Zarco and Teixeira rushed to claim it for Portugal in 1419.

We have the benefit of a very powerful lighthouse, 123 meters high and visible from 29 nautical miles, to help us identify the passage south of Porto Santo and north of Ilhas

Desertas to approach the largest of the island group, Madeira Grande.

... still later October 25
Current position: 33° 04´ N, 16° 05´ W
Making 8 knots on a course of 180 degrees magnetic

It's now well into darkness, and we are in no particular hurry because we'll reach port in the wee hours of the morning and dare not go into the marina, where we have to lay alongside other boats. Nobody welcomes a boat alongside at 2 A.M., so we'll anchor outside the harbor breakwater and go in at a civilized hour, after we've had a snooze.

This has been a fast passage and we're here about a day earlier than I had anticipated. We now have more time to explore Madeira or may opt for more time in the Canaries if the crew wishes to push on early.

Much will depend on whether we can get into the marina; it is very busy this time of year. If we can't get a spot, we'll have to set up the inflatable dinghy and the new outboard which hasn't been broken in yet. We have no gas on board, so we have to figure a way to go in and pick some up; then there's the inconvenience of timing the dinghy runs in to shore and out to the boat. I faxed the harbormaster through Inmarsat to let him know when we're to arrive, but there's no telling if the message reached him or if it will make any difference.

All are happy to think of walking where there's no rolling about or following seas breaking over the back of one's neck. Rich King anticipated the island visit by bringing a 1973(!) *National Geographic* with great photos, and we also have *The Royal Cruising Club Pilotage Foundation Atlantic Island Guide.* This information has stimulated land-lust among our unshowered, salt-encrusted crew.

On the navigation front, we didn't fetch the island approach on our long, broad-reaching starboard tack. A port tack due south will position us to fetch the harbor approach. Soon the wind will be on our starboard quarter for the last 50 nautical miles to Funchal, the capital and main port of Ilha da Madeira.

Thursday October 26
1326 GMT
Funchal, Madeira, Portugal

We came safely to anchor at 0400 GMT, after scouting the possibility of going into the marina. The wind eased as we sailed into the lee of Madeira. The city was absolutely alight, glowing like a Christmas celebration. Hydroelectric sites generate about ten percent of their electricity; the rest is from oil. The streets, which snake up the mountainside, are lined with lights and make the harbor so bright that we could see clearly on deck, under an overcast sky.

The inner harbor marina is full, and too small for us anyway, so we anchored out. We spent hours this morning unpacking and assembling the dinghy and outboard motor. All is in order now. A neighbor took the crew ashore to fetch gasoline. Lee must go shopping, so we want to have our launch running within the hour.

… later October 26
1547 GMT
Funchal, Madeira, Portugal

In the process of going through customs I asked about all of the bright lights. Although it's expensive to keep them lit, it's done to stimulate tourism and please the visitors who are here or coming in on big cruise liners. I was most disappointed.

The newly donated outboard, four-stroke engine runs as smooth as glass! It's the one Ted Kaye, Mystic Seaport shipyard stockroom manager, shipped over to Gosport, where we picked it up when we returned from Amsterdam. We're thrilled to have it.

Sunday October 29
2120 GMT
Funchal, Madeira, Portugal

Tomorrow morning we leave for the Canaries after four days here in Madeira — just long enough for the crew to have a grand time getting to know the city and some of the island's more remote spots. The weather has been perfect. Two groups on two different days rented cars and drove the north coastal road, which has dramatic mountain passes between the north and south sides. The mountains are relatively young and volcanic, so they have a brutal jaggedness and forbidding presence. This makes the extent of development and settlement over the centuries seem astonishing. Homes all over the south-facing mountainsides sit on terraces cut out of rock, a feature of almost everything established by man. It's the only way anything can be built here.

Footpaths, roads, aqueducts, farm fields, and all other forms of development are possible only through terraced construction on these steep slopes. The entire island was once covered in woods; a fire set to clear the land burned for six years! There are still extensively forested areas high in the mountains.

Because of daily rain, which is generated at high altitudes where the mountains seem perpetually shrouded, the island is lush and agriculturally rich. There are banana plantations and grapes for the famed Madeira wine. The area is also known for producing beautiful embroidery. Approximately 75,000 women, young and old, are engaged in this cottage industry. However, tourism is the primary source of income.

Christine and Rich traveled to a mountain peak where they walked and met some interesting people. Here are some words from Christine about the day's adventure:

"Our fantastic stay in Madeira culminated for me in a wonderful hike. Rich and I took a bus to Monte, a town 1,650 meters up the hill. The ride was hair-raising, with the massive bus careening around hairpin turns and not slowing for blind curves, simply honking its horn and trusting that cars would pull over. We made it safely and engaged a taxi to take us to Pico Arieiro which, at about 5,000 feet, was where we'd begin our hike. Rich and I realized that we didn't have enough money to take the taxi back, but our driver was merciful and agreed to pick us up at five P.M. for ten American dollars.

"The altitude was so great that we were in the clouds, so we didn't see spectacular views. We didn't feel cheated though; the landscape is so varied that there are always interesting things to see. It felt as if we were on some fictional planet, with strange rocks, red clay, lichens, and many unfamiliar plants. We saw a few birds, we heard sheep and goats and saw about ten fellow hikers, as well as rabbit hunters and their dogs. We hiked up and down for about four hours, almost reaching the highest point on Madeira.

"Armando, our taxi driver, reappeared as promised, and drove us all the way back to Funchal at a discount. He even stopped at a bar to have us try the traditional Madeiran drink Puncha. After discovering we were Americans, Armando gave us his views on President Clinton and Monica. He told us about his son, revealed that he had been a taxi driver for 30 years, and said he misses his old Datsun. He's not as happy with a Mercedes, which is what all the cabbies drive now. We showed him *Brilliant* at anchor, bade him farewell, and made it to the boat just in time for a chicken parmesan dinner."

Monday October 30
1251 GMT
Position at 1200 GMT: 32° 20´ N, 16° 51´ W

We are on our way to Tenerife. We are making 8 knots on a course of 180° magnetic, with moderate seas of five feet and force-4 winds on the port quarter. All is rather pleasant. Madeira is barely visible astern.

Tuesday October 31
1503 GMT
Position at 1200 GMT: 29° 15´ N, 16° 13´W
Making 8 knots on a course of 175° magnetic, with three-foot seas and a force-4 east wind under an overcast sky

Tenerife, with volcanic mountains as high as 12,000 feet, is in sight. Our ETA is about 2200 GMT. We expect to go into Marina del Atlantico, which is in the harbor area called Darsena de los Llanos, the southernmost of the marinas in Santa Cruz de Tenerife. None of this will be certain until we are actually received, as we've learned from experience.

The crew is relaxed, reading travel guides to Tenerife and other islands. "Cruise ship *Brilliant*" is a happy one.

... later October 31
2227 GMT (1727 EST)
Santa Cruz, Tenerife, Canary Islands, Spain

We arrived safely and in good spirits in Tenerife at 1930 GMT. We are stern to a concrete dock that is inboard of the largest breakwater I've ever seen, clearly designed to hold out the most raging of tempests. We've finished dinner; some of the crew have already collapsed in deep sleep. Others are on deck, listening to music and contemplating going ashore.

Wednesday November 1
0939 GMT
Santa Cruz, Tenerife, Canary Islands, Spain

We're starting our field day, airing the boat and its contents after a good night's rest and breakfast aboard. The sun's warmth already embraces us at 9 A.M.; any notions of gloom evaporate into the clear sky. No wonder the lightest hearts live in the south. By noon all ship's work will be a memory, and we'll be answering the call of shoreside adventure. Most of the crew plan to stay for a few days longer; there's much to see in very little time! How could we be less than grateful for this experience?

Monday November 6
Santa Cruz, Tenerife, Canary Islands, Spain

We've been working hard on maintenance for the last four days and have two fresh coats of varnish on most areas; one on others. Six are aboard, all pitching in to make things happen. A couple more days' work and we'll have her looking pretty spiffy.

Wednesday November 8
Santa Cruz, Tenerife, Canary Islands, Spain

All is well here. I feel very good about all the fine work that has been done by the crew pitching in with full energy. Rich King, Dan Bregman, Donna Kelly, Christine Alberi, and Lee Wacker have all been going at it like champs. We'll be ready for the Atlantic crossing to Antigua without a doubt.

Monday November 13
1549 GMT
Santa Cruz, Tenerife, Canary Islands, Spain

We're back in the maintenance routine after a free weekend. Rich King is off traveling until late in the week. Dan Bregman and I remained aboard, but Christine and Lee stayed at a hotel one night this weekend to have some time off the boat and enjoy a real bed, clean showers, prolonged sleep, and an escape from harbor odors.

Because of heavy rain on Saturday and a reverse of wind direction, the harbor filled with sewer water and run-off from the land and drain pipes. The marina was loaded with floating trash and permeated by a very unpleasant smell. But a change in wind combined with tidal flushing has returned clearer water and more pleasant air.

We'll take on fuel Wednesday. We've decided to carry 50 gallons of diesel fuel on deck to give us more motoring range in case we run into light air. This precaution should give us about 250 additional miles of motoring for a total of about 750 miles, depending on how much fuel we burn charging batteries and refrigeration. It should increase our odds of arriving in Antigua on time.

There are some groups of boats sailing across about the same time we are. One, called the ARC, consists of about 250 boats which are organized to do the crossing "in company." They are departing on the 19th. Another smaller group leaves slightly earlier, the 17th I think. We'll likely be a little faster than some of these boats, so we think we'll have some company along the way with our departure on the 20th. Of course, we need to remember that when we raced across from Halifax with a fleet of 40, we hardly ever saw another boat until we reached the English coast. Regardless, it's a little comforting to know there'll be so many other boats out there within a few hundred miles of our position.

I've been studying weather maps for the areas we'll be sailing through: about 19 degrees north to 20 degrees north. It seems there may be light air as we approach the west. A low-pressure area has been hanging to the west of a high in the Azores, and it looks as if there could be some light air south of the low — especially if that low persists or drifts north, or if another low with the same northward drift replaces it. We'll need a strategy for communications regarding weather because I don't think we'll be able to get maps from the weather fax. Our equipment's reception has been very bad here and will get worse until we get closer to NOAA's radio tower.

Jan Miles from *Pride of Baltimore II* has offered to help us plan routing via Inmarsat and I may take him up on that. Perhaps Don Treworgy at Mystic Seaport could watch the NOAA maps and let me know where the friendly air might be. We're waiting to learn who will be the new president of the United States.

Saturday November 18
2258 GMT
Santa Cruz, Tenerife, Canary Islands, Spain

The crew has done well catching up on maintenance and preparing *Brilliant* for the crossing to Antigua. Dan, Rich, and Christine have put in many hours painting, varnishing, cleaning, replacing, and fixing. Before she left, Donna Kelly gave us some of her time. Lee has been cleaning but is mostly busy with the enormous task of provisioning.

Details are vitally important. For example, we inspected the rigging elements for chafe and signs of fatigue. I went aloft to check the upper rig details on both masts and found one very significant shackle had lost its mousing and its pin had backed out most of the way. That shackle happened to hold the main lower backstay — a rather important feature for holding up the rig when sailing downwind! *Brilliant's* bottom had become quite fouled from all the harbors we've visited, so it was high time to give it a scrub. It took a local diver two sessions to get it clean. That's worth half a knot of boat speed, which is a lot when you're covering 3,000 miles.

We took on fuel yesterday and were lucky to have a diligent harbormaster who organized tax-free fuel for the many boats seeking to fill up for the crossing. We received 100 gallons for about $140, a bargain at European prices. We have 54 gallons on deck in fourteen containers, making us the smallest container ship in the harbor.

Now some words from Rich King, who enjoyed an adventure on Lanzarote, a nearby island in the Canary group:

"I walked about two hours to Samara, on a downhill dirt road. Except for a little cold and rain, it was lovely. As I approached a bend where I'd see the whole valley, a squall came through below. I saw a colossal, whole-sky, full-arc, two-pots-of-gold rainbow, with the start of a second on the left. An old farmer with a wheel barrow was working, facing the other way. I wanted to shout 'Look at that rainbow!' so he'd turn around. But I didn't.

"As I walked down into the valley, the rainbow faded and the squalls edged over me. I felt good about the land getting rain. People waved from the few houses I passed. Dogs barked at me — maybe because I wore a towel over my head like a shawl. Once, when crouched in the lee of a sandstone wall to get out of the rain, I looked out on the dry bald hills, the cliff, the sea, the beach, and though I was cold and wet I thought, 'Well, here I am in Lanzarote, in the Canary Islands. I like the xylophone sound of rain thrumming on a can and soon I will sail across the Atlantic with the help of these same winds, on a most beautiful and cared-for schooner that is more than 40 years older than I.'"

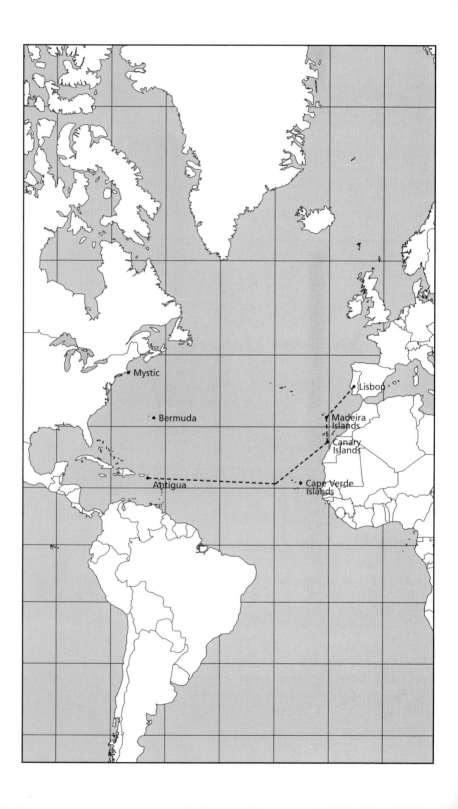

Mystic

Bermuda

Lisbon

Madeira
Islands

Canary
Islands

Antigua

Cape Verde
Islands

Chapter Three

Heavenly Crossing
November 20, 2000 - December 7, 2000

The pace slows ... we remove our foul-weather gear ... follow the trade winds and the stars ... feed on fresh fish ... nearly break our own a record ... and make landfall in sunny Antigua.

Monday November 20
1201 GMT
Santa Cruz, Tenerife, Canary Islands, Spain

We'll be casting off and under way to Antigua in about 20 minutes. The 84-hour weather prognosis looks good. We've found a good weather map on the Web at *http://www.nlmoc.navy.mil/newpage/blend*. It's the U.S. Navy's information on surface wind for the southern section of the North Atlantic. I'll ask Don Treworgy to monitor this from Mystic, so he can advise me. I'll see what success I have receiving weather maps via fax.

We'll be in contact with *Geronimo* (a 74-foot vessel custom-designed by Ted Hood for the St. George's School At-Sea program) daily at 0803 GMT by SSB radio. They left the nearby island of Gomera this morning, which will put them more than a hundred miles ahead of us, but it'll be good to have contact. *Geronimo* calls St. George's daily, so if our Inmarsat goes

Crew List
November 19 - December 9
Tenerife, Canary Islands, Spain - Antigua

Professional Crew

George Moffett, captain
Ledyard, CT

Christine Alberi, mate
Summit, NJ

Rich King, watch leader
Mystic, CT

Lee Wacker, cook and medical technician
Old Lyme, CT

Cadets

Daniel Evan Bregman
Old Mystic, CT

Cipperly Anne Good
St. Albans, VT

Hamilton Scott Moore
New Canaan, CT

Wade C. Smith
Mystic, CT

Alyssa Todd Stover
N. Stonington, CT

David Evan Thomas
New York, NY

down, we may be able to relay messages through them. It's good to know we'll have company.

Geronimo does not fly a spinnaker so I feel confident that we'll stay within range of each other for a while.[1] On the Tall Ships race across, *Maiden* (the Whitbread ocean racing sloop) didn't use a spinnaker and *Brilliant* sailed a bit better downwind than she could.

Antigua is at about 17° N. Our present plan is to sail toward 20° N and 30° W, after which we'll probably sail south a little further, to 18° N perhaps. Then we'll see how the winds are shaping up. The trade winds may be better to the south, so we may want to dip down to 16° N. We should be able to learn something about wind conditions from the ARC fleet. They're sailing several days ahead of us and will be communicating with each other on SSB radio.

We've just completed our safety discussions and line drills, and are about to start raising our anchor and 300-foot chain, which have been in the water for three weeks!

... later November 20
1726 GMT

We're just clearing Tenerife's southwest corner and will soon be in open ocean again, with a following sea and lots of rocking and rolling.

Tuesday November 21
0939 GMT
Position at 0900 GMT: 26° 22′ N, 17° 29′ W
Making 6.3 knots (motoring), on a course of 245° magnetic

Weather information from Don Treworgy indicates northeast winds at 20 knots; unfortunately it doesn't correspond with what we're experiencing. We had a good northeast breeze departing Tenerife and through much of the night as we sailed a course of about 210° magnetic. But we now have

---

1 A spinnaker would give *Geronimo* extra speed and increase her separation from *Brilliant*.

no wind and have been motoring for about two hours. We are worried to be motoring so early in the game.

Our weather fax reception is very poor but produces readable maps. We haven't been able to get maps that cover the area down to 20° N. No one feels that we'll find 25 knots anywhere nearby.

I spoke with *Geronimo* this morning but we could barely understand each other. They're about 30 nautical miles north of us and 60 nautical miles to our west. We don't know what kind of wind they're experiencing; with the size of this high, I'd be surprised if they have more wind than we do.

We've already talked about stopping at the Cape Verde Islands for fuel, but we have hardly enough fuel to get us there. We hope this calm will pass soon. Unfortunately, nothing happens very quickly in the weather around here this time of year. Some of the boats in Tenerife are waiting to depart until January, when the trade winds fill. We waited as long as we could to avoid the hurricane season (which ends in late November), but our schedule prevents waiting any longer. We'll see if this calm will pass. Not sure what we'll do if it doesn't.

... later November 21
1540 GMT
Position at 1200 GMT: 26° 10´ N, 17° 39´ W
Noon-to-noon run: 161 nautical miles over the bottom
Currently making 5 to 6 knots, on a course of 200° magnetic under sail – after motoring for about 3.5 hours this morning
Winds are from the northeast at about 10 knots

Sextants are everywhere! Lee Wacker shot Polaris this morning and worked up the numbers to get our line of position. Her calculations came very close to our position according to the GPS. Rich King just completed a running fix, using a morning sun sight and a noon sun sight for latitude. We may give the *Selected Stars Volume of H.O. 249*[2] a go this evening.

---

2   A reference used for navigation, which provides information on a recommended set of stars that will be most visible and useful for navigation at sunrise or sunset at a given time and latitude.

Everything indicates that we are where we think we are.

Calm seas and bright light have made us all cheerful, but more speed and a better heading would be much appreciated. We're not "westing" as much as we'd like, but we stay on this heading because we think going south on this tack is better than west on the other. General wisdom seems to favor getting south before sailing too far west.

Now, some of Dan Bregman's impressions:

"After almost three long, hard weeks sanding, scraping, varnishing, and painting, we're all glad to be under way again. Of course we did other things to occupy our time on Tenerife. For example, we attended the grand opening of the first Irish pub on the island. The pints were on the house and we didn't understand anything anyone said because it was all in Spanish. It was a blast!

"Wade Smith, Alyssa Stover, and I went to the top of the tallest mountain in Spain. It's actually a dormant volcano. Christine Alberi and Lee Wacker had also done this hike. All along the trail there were holes in the rocks, with hot sulfur-smelling gases seeping out. None of us had ever seen anything like it.

"We just set our first fishing line. We're eagerly anticipating the five-hundred-pound tuna that I promised the others. If it turns out to be a bit smaller, we'd still be happy."

Wednesday November 22
1521 GMT
Position at 1200 GMT: 25° 19′ N, 19° 43′ W
Making 6 to 7 knots on a course of 245° to 255° magnetic
Wind is out of the north-northwest at 10 to 15 knots

I sent a message to the manufacturer of our weather fax, seeking technical support. We get narrow bands of staggered reception, and have to "cut and paste" to read our faxes. The problem developed several months ago on the Atlantic crossing. Frank Bohlen tried to find the cause, but it remained elusive even after Frank and I both studied the manual. A fault may have developed in the software or a little magic box called the demodulator.

We've set all of our 3,000+ square feet of sail. Our golliwobbler, large reacher, and full main are pulling us along on a beam reach as we play frequent little wind shifts to keep *Brilliant* moving. We're starting to see and overtake various smaller vessels which are in the ARC fleet of 250 boats.

We couldn't reach *Geronimo* this morning so I emailed St. George's school, proposing alternative radio channels. The school should email back through Don at Mystic. We're using these go-betweens because Steve Connett, *Geronimo's* captain and founder of the At-Sea program, says we can't communicate ship-to-ship with Inmarsat, although I've done it with other ships.

All's well, we're just not moving fast enough. Lee is already working tomorrow's Thanksgiving feast. As always, her cooking has been superb. Everyone raves about it. Christine and Rich are doing superb jobs of leading their watches. There is great harmony in the group, with personalities fitting together well.

We had five sextants out last night shooting stars. With the help of the *Selected Stars Volume of H.O. 249*, we looked for Mirfak, Hamal, Diphda, Fomalhaut, Altair, Vega, and Deneb, and had some success. Jupiter and Saturn are very bright as they rise. Venus is so bright in the southwest that it casts a moon-like glow on the water as it sets. The sky was stunning, with streaks of falling stars. We watched Orion rise and anticipated the rise of Sirius. Rich achieved a good LAN[3] today and is shooting the afternoon sun now. We will not get lost.

... later November 22
1830 GMT

We went onto starboard tack yesterday evening after concluding that port tack wasn't giving us enough westing. We were starting to see ships, so we felt we were too close to the African coast. That turned out to be a good decision because a northwester has come in. We're presently making 7 to 8 knots comfortably.

---

3   Local apparent noon, the time when the sun reaches the day's maximum height, as observed from the ship.

Thursday November 23
1053 GMT
Current position: 23° 41′ N, 22° 03′ W
Making about 7 knots on a heading of 208° magnetic (197° true)
Sailing on port tack with northeast winds of 10 to 15 knots and two foot seas

Thanksgiving greetings from the southeastern North Atlantic. We're working our way toward the Cape Verde Islands before catching the real trade winds that await us about 100 miles south.

Had contact this morning with *Geronimo*. They're about 60 nautical miles to our southwest with plenty of wind, making 8 knots on a course of 200° magnetic. Conversations between the ARC boats indicate there's more wind coming soon. *Geronimo* motored for 36 hours to work her way southwest to get the wind. We've motored only about eight hours; all things considered, we feel pretty good to be where we are, having used only about ten gallons of fuel.

We anticipate that the winds will bend more to the east as we move into the major bands of the transatlantic trades. A boat at 19° N, 27° W reports that it had 20- to 30-knot winds this morning! This confirms the forecast that Don sent yesterday from the Navy Web site. Herb Hilgenberg has broadcast a favorable forecast, predicting good air south of 23° N for the next four days. We pulled some good, clear maps off our weather fax after eliminating the problem caused by the energy-saving software in our laptop. These maps give us information as far south as 20° N, so they're of some use. But they're not as clear or useful as the Navy's charts for the southern area of the North Atlantic.

We're looking forward to Lee's feast and to stronger trade winds from the east. The watermaker is working fine and we've topped up all the tanks. There's enough food aboard for another 30 days, so if we can keep the old girl afloat we should make it; if the trades hold, we should be on time.

If it's possible for a boat to suffer navigation overkill, it's happening on *Brilliant*! Lots of good stuff is going on in the sky. Rich's morning Polaris sight yielded a position line within one mile of our actual latitude. Star sights taken last night confirmed that the government satellites are very reliable!

... later November 23
1240 GMT
Position at 1200 GMT: 23° 32´ N, 22° 05´ W
Making 8 knots on a course of 200° magnetic
Wind from the northeast at 15 knots with seas 2 to 3 feet

Brilliant is moving very well under full, light-air canvas. Andy Halsey and his crew of sailmakers should know that the 1.5-ounce reacher is a tremendous sail – a real workhorse. It'll make all the difference on this leg. In these trade winds it really pulls, and it's so easy to set.

... later November 23
2137 GMT

We had a superb dinner and entertainment – full-out self-indulgence. We've been enjoying the rich tapestry of life and saw no reason to let up. Could we be thankful enough? Here's Alyssa to tell you about it:

"Thanksgiving on the water was a new experience. The talents and creativity of the crew made it memorable. Since food is the main focus of Thanksgiving Day, we were especially thrilled with Lee's efforts. She began preparing last night. The smells of baking pies wafting up from the galley nearly drove the night watches wild. This morning brought more temptations, with perfectly round home-made rolls waiting to be popped into the oven. Some of the morning watch pitched in to peel and cut up potatoes, which Lee whisked away to the galley.

"Rich, ever humorous and upbeat, suggested that one watch dress up as Pilgrims and the other as Native Americans. With few props on board, resourcefulness was the key to a convincing costume. Rich also felt it was a good day for arts-and-crafts, so he brought an odd assortment of materials up on deck. From a wool sock, a towel, several dusting brushes, a red scarf, sunglasses and some twine, emerged a fine-looking turkey! We now have a mascot for the boat and a good conversation piece.

"As dinnertime drew near, we withdrew to our bunks to don the proper dress for the occasion. The Pilgrims relied heavily on black clothing for a somber look, wide-brimmed rain hats with belts around the crowns, and plenty of buckles prominently displayed in proper Pilgrim style. The Native-American maidens wore their hair in braids, and one chief tied a dusting brush to his head to simulate a Mohawk haircut.

"When Lee ushered us down to fill our plates, there was turkey, stuffing, mashed potatoes, honeyed squash, gravy, steamed broccoli, cranberry sauce, and the perfect rolls. For our vegetarian on board, Lee created a sliced seitan dish that matched any turkey for tastiness. We ate up on deck together, with people taking turns at the wheel so everyone could get their fill – and fill we did. We loudly praised the cook.

"For a little exercise before dessert, we decided to jibe. We hauled away, made fast, eased off, and got ready for pie. We devoured apple and pumpkin pies, with some Pilgrims and Natives going back for thirds! Even the cook had to admit that the pies were excellent, but added that they made her feel a little homesick. We all agreed. But we also conceded that it's awfully nice to be where we are."

Friday November 24
1227 GMT
Position at 1200 GMT: 22° 49′ N, 25° 05′ W
Making 8.5 knots on a course of 230° magnetic
2037 GMT
Current position: 21° 47′ N, 25° 49′ W

We are well into the trade winds. Geronimo has slightly stronger wind 115 miles south of us.

We have plenty of wind now, more than 20 knots out of the east. We're making good speed and have shortened sail. We plan to continue a southwest course until we get south of 21° N, then perhaps we'll tack. Eight-foot following seas make helming difficult, even with a reef in the main.

Saturday November 25
1331 GMT
Position at 1200 GMT: 20° 27′ N, 27° 35′ W
Making 8.5 knots on a course of 235° magnetic
Winds out of the east at about 20 knots, up to 25 knots through the night

We covered more than 200 nautical miles on each of the last two days, with a two-day noon-to-noon total of 409 nautical miles and 583 nautical miles over the past three days. We've sailed 883 nautical miles since our noon departure from Tenerife five days ago.

Antigua is about 1,950 nautical miles ahead. *Brilliant* is presently under reefed main, fore, fisherman, and #1 jib. Following seas are presenting a challenge to the helm. We anticipate lighter air ahead, based on information from the weather maps. We're heading southwest, as recommended.

Geronimo, which was west of us by 70 nautical miles at 8 A.M., will be laying about the same course as ours – perhaps a little more west since she is sailing a bit more off the wind, with only her jib and no main. We had a good clear radio contact with her.

There has been lots of chatter with "Gary" on radio frequency 8101 Khz where some ARC fleet participants check in with wind reports. Gary offers weather advice based on these reports from the ARC fleet combined with information from official sources.

We're enjoying the Thanksgiving leftovers. Lee, of course, can make even leftovers taste special. The crew is gaining weight as the ship loses hers. We have glorious sailing, but lots of sleep deprivation due to motion, noise, and unfamiliar sleep cycles – four or six hours on; four or six off. Waves occasionally come aboard, dampening the sea's romance slightly. Flying fish have been landing on deck and flying head-high among the on-watch crew, causing mild surprise. One of those that landed on deck is now being towed astern on the end of a hook. We hope to catch something bigger.

... later November 25
2116 GMT

Don Treworgy's weather report suggests we head south – and so we are. But the temptation to head west is enormous because the velocity made good to our destination is so much greater on that tack.

Sunday November 26
1236 GMT
Position at 1200 GMT: 18° 01´ N, 29° 49´ W
Making 7.5 knots on a course of 230° magnetic

Noon-to-noon distances over the bottom[4] starting with our departure from Tenerife:

Nov. 20 - 21	161 nautical miles
Nov. 21 - 22	140 nautical miles
Nov. 22 - 23	174 nautical miles
Nov. 23 - 24	205 nautical miles
Nov. 24 - 25	203 nautical miles
Nov. 25 - 26	196 nautical miles

This morning we learned that *Brilliant* and *Geronimo* are on almost the same latitude, but that she's 57 nautical miles west of us. We've agreed to tack for some westing when we reach 18° N. If we're forced north, we'll tack back to our present course (if the wind permits) because we don't want to sail out of stronger wind, which is forecast to be south of 19° N. It is tempting to continue southwest, but I'm not sure if the wind will be any better than it is now at 18° N.

We've just enjoyed a tremendous lunch. Everyone's on deck, waiting to tack.

---

4 All such distances are read from the GPS log. "Distance over the bottom" is a measure of the true number of miles traveled. Distance over the bottom includes miles that are added because of tacking and jibing.

Monday November 27
1625 GMT
Position at 1200 GMT: 18° 18′ N, 32° 24′ W
Noon-to-noon distance: 161 nautical miles
Making 7.5 to 8.6 knots on a heading of 270° to 280° magnetic
Wind is 15 to 20 knots out of the northeast, having freshened after many hours of light air

Brilliant is making hardly a noise because the seas are only a couple of feet high. When below, you can hardly tell she's moving. When the seas come in however, the rolling generates a lot of creaking as the panels work in the bulkhead frames. You can put your fingers along the panel and frame joints and feel the motion that makes the noise – the motion of a living ship as she responds to tremendous pressure from the elements. We sleep comfortably when it doesn't creak; less so when there is lots of motion. The recent relative quiet leads to healthy dispositions. The need for sleep is unrelenting.

All the watches did a great job playing the wind shifts through the night, heading up when the wind eased and falling off as it freshened. They did the same for direction shifts – and there were many. This is done by watching the luff of the big reacher (which is set flying; not hanked to the stay) and watching the windsock for changes in apparent wind. When the luff folds in, you're too close to the wind; when the sock points toward the bow or the sail collapses in the lee of the other sails, you're too far off the wind. This is the only way to keep the boat moving in light air, which in this case was about 10 knots for most of yesterday.

We took more celestial sights, with Rich getting a good position by crossing a Polaris line with a Jupiter line. Yesterday's LAN worked well. Cipperly and Dan shot the sun at LAN today and Ham calculated the time for the LAN, all under Rich's enthusiastic supervision. We've done a couple of compass deviation checks: one by using the shadow of a vertical pin at the center of the compass card, another by calculating the bearing of Venus with our Celesticomp. At one point Venus was setting just ahead of us, so we changed course a little bit to line up our masts with the planet and then checked the true bearing of Venus, adjusting for local variation. As in the past, we found zero deviation. We are blessed with a reliable compass.

Christine organized a very effective field day; major cleaning and polishing led to feeling that *Brilliant* is a much-loved ship. Taking care of *Brilliant* feels like giving thanks to her.

We saw a couple of pilot whales early this morning. Dolphins and sea birds have occasionally appeared, seemingly from out of nowhere.

Now some words from Rich King:

"The creaking in the main cabin sounds like you have put your head under the seat of a wicker rocking chair in which your heaviest uncle sits, rocks, lounges, then readjusts. At the end of *Brilliant's* bowsprit is a monel bow pulpit, a seat that faces the deck. Cipperly is sitting there, facing aft, watching the ship move. The bobstay dips into the water, occasionally scattering a patch of flying fish. Above her the reacher billows, so light and thin that she can see sunlight through the seams. The reacher "hunts" the wind, carefully whooshing back and forth to fill with breeze. Cipperly has not seen one boat on the horizon today.

"We've created some new sails for the vessel's inventory: the tons'l, pens'l, windows'l, and hans'l."

Tuesday November 28
1428 GMT
Positions at 1200 GMT: 17° 58′ N, 35° 57′ W
Making 9 knots on a course of 285° magnetic
Wind out of the east-northeast at 15 to 20 knots
Swells: 10 feet or more
Noon-to-noon distance: 204 nautical miles

We're nearly half way through the passage with about 1,450 nautical miles to go. We'll celebrate the halfway mark before dinner tonight, with "swizzle," a nonalcoholic but light-headed drink brewed in the darkest chambers below deck by the cook.

We spoke with *Geronimo* this morning. They are 75 nautical miles west of us on almost the same parallel of latitude. This is another staggeringly beautiful day with a rising glass [barometer]. We have 30.20 inches of mercury, up from 30.16 inches yesterday.

I pulled in several NOAA weather faxes for our area but they were fuzzy and weak. We've been able to get good surface analysis charts, however. A large high-pressure center runs east-and-west to the north of us, a finding confirmed by the Inmarsat text forecast. Don's prediction of 20-knot easterly winds at this latitude was right on the money. We are doing very well with weather information from these various sources, especially the Navy Web page and Don's interpretation. We missed Herb Hilgenberg's forecast last night but will try to catch it this evening .

The sails provided by Andy Halsey and his loft in Mystic are great, especially the 1.5-ounce reacher. It holds up well to wind speeds as high as 20 knots on the quarter, making it possible for us to sail downwind with a full main providing a balanced helm.

The crew are taking noon sights to get our LAN. Rich is on deck with Cipperly and Ham doing LAN sights. Christine is at the helm, happy and radiant. There's a lot of boat motion but she's holding a steady course. The watermaker is keeping our tanks full and the crew bathed – Don and Angie Robinson [who donated the equipment] are very popular with the crew.

Wednesday November 29
1312 GMT
Position at 1200 GMT: 18° 52′ N, 39° 20′ W
Noon-to-noon distance traveled: 203 nautical miles
Wind is east at 15 knots

Rich and Christine are keeping us all going on navigation and other subjects. Just minutes ago we caught our first fish, a mahimahi (dolphin fish) about 42 inches long. It put up a good struggle, but in the end we're having fresh fish for dinner. Lee is quite excited. Rich has been given the job of cleaning it.

Now some observations from Dave Thomas:

"When we started this passage, the crew were sharply divided into two groups: 'veterans' of *Brilliant's* 2000 voyage and 'novices' to the trip. Observations by the novices often met with ill-concealed condescension from the veterans.

"'Boy, this boat sure rolls at sea!' said the novices. 'This is nothing! You should'a' been with us in the Irish sea!' said one of the veterans.

"'Boy, it's sure noisy in the cabin!' said the novices. Indeed, the flexing bulkheads can sound like the Chicago Bears tap-dancing on bubble wrap. 'This is nothing! You should'a' been with us on the transatlantic crossing!' said the veterans.

"'We ARE on a transatlantic crossing,' said the novices.

"A few days into the passage, the wind and seas picked up. One night both watches dressed in full battle gear – hooded and booted, with much clinking of shackles from the safety harnesses. Together, we engaged in combat with the elements. *Brilliant* corkscrewed down quartering swells, and spray occasionally hit the crew crouched in the cockpit. The 'novices' paid their dues, and ideas about status began to erode.

"We've been enjoying fair weather and moderate seas. Last night we enjoyed 'cocktails' and canapés on deck like inshore pleasure cruisers. We each sacrificed a piece of personal gear to propitiate Neptune and celebrate the mid-point of our trip. By day we've seen pilot whales, shearwaters, and hundreds of flying fish; one hit Rich kamikaze-style. At night we're stunned by the sight of falling stars – some explode like flares in orange and green bursts.

"Although I envy the veterans' heroic tales of a glory-filled eastbound crossing, I'm quite content to be making this trip under gentlemanly downwind conditions."

Thursday November 30
1514 GMT
Position at 1200 GMT: 17° 18′ N, 41° 36′ W
Noon-to-noon distance: 186 nautical miles
Making 8 knots

We sailed to 19° N, experienced lighter air as predicted, and tacked onto port to do some southing. Jibing on these long legs is such a pleasure. Every day feels like a great, loving gift.

I've been interested to see how close a celestial navigation sight (reduced by tables) comes to the Celesticomp. Yesterday's experiment yielded a significant difference of about 5 miles. I started with all the same input and couldn't find any math errors in my work. It's one of those frustrating things that has no tangible solution – a bit like theology.

I've figured out how to do a running fix with the Celesticomp, combining sun, planet, and moon sights and working those sights back to get a fixed position from earlier in the day. My result came within one mile of our position according to the GPS. The Celesticomp advises on the difference between the estimated position (also known as dead reckoning) and what it concludes is the actual fix, eliminating erroneous LOPs. It's an amazing gadget, and it takes mental focus to learn its tricks.

I feel sure we could keep quite accurate positions and make a precise landfall even if all of our electronics went down (including the Celesticomp) assuming we had visibility. Don Treworgy's celestial navigation course has generated so much enthusiasm. He's with us in many ways!

This morning we caught another fish, probably a mahi-mahi, but it got away as we slowly pulled it in. At a strong 8 knots, I think we're going a bit fast for fishing.

Now some insights from Christine, who has this boat sailing sweetly:

"Looking back in the log book this morning I discovered that *Brilliant* has sailed almost 9,000 miles since the beginning of the season! It's hard to get one's brain around that thought, especially when you're focused on a daunting 3,000 mile transatlantic leg!

"The weather gods have smiled upon us at last. These last few weeks have been a spectacular joy of blue skies, warm night watches, flying fish, and stars. The wind and waves are finally at our back and for the first time we're sailing without full foul weather gear.

"The crew have been teasing me about my many sailing superstitions. I tied our mahimahi's tail to the end of the bowsprit for good fortune, I've banned whistling on board, and I keep rapping my knuckles on teak and mahogany. Hopefully the weather gods who are beaming down on us right now will take this message as a thank you for the nice weather, instead of a jinx."

Friday December 1
1411 GMT
Position at 1200 GMT: 17° 45´ N, 44° 42´ W
Noon-to-noon distance: 198 nautical miles
On port tack, making 8 knots on a course of 230° magnetic
Wind is from east-by-north (78°), blowing 15 to 20 knots

Our GPS is running, but we've returned to traditional methods of navigation. Those who are navigating on the two watches aren't allowed to look at the GPS. Christine and Rich are doing a good job of teaching.

In today's navigation drill we towed our taffrail log, which has been on the boat for decades. We used it to calculate distance. That, with our corrected compass course for direction, enabled us to establish our position by dead reckoning. We checked our results against running fixes taken from sun sights.

We tried to calibrate the taffrail log by comparing its reading with that of our GPS over the course of 80 nautical miles. We found that it reads 0.6 nautical miles more than the GPS. Because of current, the GPS reading should be higher than the towed log's – but we found the reverse, so we don't know how precise the log is.

We did a star fix last night, using Vega, Fomalhaut, Jupiter, and Venus. We'll use several sun sights that were taken this morning, together with our noon sights, to determine running fixes after we get a late afternoon sun sight. The crew members are starting to fight for use of the *Nautical Almanac* – there have been bloody scenes and unkind language. Let's hope our ship is not found adrift at sea with all hands missing and torn-out pages of the *Nautical Almanac* scattered about!

Now some words from Cipperly Good:

"I came on *Brilliant* with two goals in mind: to be able to competently steer a course and to be able to use a sextant. Well, I have succeeded! I can steer *Brilliant* even with the compass covered, which is part of my watch leader's tough-love training. I have also successfully shot the sun with a sextant. My reading was only five nautical miles off – not bad, considering that we're riding a roller coaster of waves. A whole library of stars are being logged in my brain!"

Saturday December 2
Position at 1200 GMT: 17° 19′ N, 47° 32′ W, about 812 nautical miles east of Antigua
Noon-to-noon distance: 203 nautical miles
On starboard tack, making 8 to 9 knots on a course of 315° magnetic (our desired course is 288° magnetic)

Seas are 5 feet, air temperature 80° F; and the sky is cloud-covered. Occasional rain is falling.

The crew is fed, watered, under-slept, and non-mutinous. Contrary to wise advice gleaned from experience, we towed a fish line alongside the taffrail log, leading to excessive inter-connectedness. The crew will be busy for hours in divorce counseling, since it seems separation is not possible. Some suspect a conspiracy to keep the crew busy. The entanglement terminates today's hope for fresh fish. With this trauma, the crew is not inspired to contribute to today's report.

Sunday December 3
1442 GMT
Position at 1200 GMT: 18° 52′ N, 50° 44′ W, a little more than 630 nautical miles east of Antigua
Noon-to-noon distance: 212 nautical miles
Sailing southwest on port tack

The 48-hour and 84-hour forecast says winds in the area just northwest of us will soon veer to the southeast. So we sailed northwest on starboard tack all day yesterday and through the night, roaring along at 9 knots, with the wind north of east. Sure enough, the wind clocked south of east this morning, near 19° N and 50° W, enabling us to jibe onto port tack with a much favored heading for Antigua. It could not have worked out better. Now we're working our way southwest with the hope we will sail into the better winds near 16° N, as forecast for tomorrow. Our progress continues to be better than anticipated.

Now some words from Ham who greatly enjoyed the dead reckoning exercise (combined with observations for fixes) of the past 48 hours (which was only temporarily interrupted by fishing):

"Over the past few days *Brilliant* has been traveling back in time. Not only are we going west from Greenwich, we're reversing the technological advancements in navigation and sailing that we relied on for the first half of our trip. First we switched from the masthead light to the more traditional side and stern lanterns. Then we turned our backs on our good friend, the Global Positioning System, to rely exclusively on dead reckoning.

"Using estimated hourly headings plus boat speed and distance determined by the taffrail log dragging off the stern, our task was to calculate where we would be over a two day period. We plotted our final GPS fix, then covered the glowing screen. If all went well, Rich King optimistically said, our dead reckoning would be within a 10-mile radius of our position according to the GPS.

"Everything did not go as planned. Somehow we managed to catch the taffrail log line on the fishing line, made a few erroneous log entries and had to jibe in the middle of the night – all of which made our task more difficult. Fortunately, we have a fleet of sextants that we used regularly to adjust our dead reckoning. And we had supervision and hints from our watch leaders. After 48 hours, we were a short seven miles off – not bad, considering."

Monday December 4
1512 GMT
Position at 1200 GMT: 17° 07′ N, 53° 38′ W
Noon-to-noon distance: 204 nautical miles; Antigua is 465 nautical miles to our west
Making 8 knots on a course of 265° magnetic

Wind is from the southeast at 15 knots. The sky is partly cloudy with some rain, and major wind shifts under the clouds.

It's 86° F in the shade and 94° F in the sun. All's well, but it's almost too hot to think.

Tuesday December 5
1528 GMT
Position at 1200 GMT: 16° 52´ N, 56° 31´ W
Noon-to-noon distance: 199 nautical miles (ouch!)
Making 8 to 9 knots on a course of 230° magnetic

Half an hour ago, we were 282 nautical miles east of
Antigua. It is hot – too hot – but with a good breeze slightly
south of east. We jibed to continue southwest because we
learned from *Geronimo* that the air is lighter to the north of us.
This morning at 0800 *Geronimo* was more than 100 nautical
miles north of us and making only 6 knots, sailing wing-and-
wing. She had motored through calms in recent hours, but is
on schedule to reach Puerto Rico by the 9th. We anticipate
reaching Antigua day after tomorrow, Thursday the 7th. We
and *Geronimo* have come across the Atlantic together, usually
within 100 nautical miles of each other.

Our crew are doing a great job of sailing the boat, averag-
ing 200.7 nautical miles a day for the last 8 days. If we make
another 200 nautical miles over the next 24 hours, we could
equal *Brilliant's* legendary 1933 run: nine 200-nautical-mile
days in a row. If I remember correctly, we averaged 207 nautical miles for seven days on the crossing to England. *Brilliant* is
a good vessel for this kind of work.

Did I mention the whales we saw a couple of days ago?
They were spectacular. We had the company of one or more
for a prolonged stretch. After swimming all around us to have
a good look, one breached close to us and shocked everyone
who happened to be watching. These weren't very big whales,
around 20 to 25 feet; the one who breached had a white belly.
Their dorsal fins were small with a distinctive hook aft. Some
thought they had square heads which I think suggests they
were pilot whales – but we don't know if pilot whales have
white undersides. We wish we had a sea mammal identifica-
tion book on board.

Wade's 28th birthday was yesterday, so we celebrated with
a grand feast last night. Rich, with his artistic talent, made a
birthday card with a cartoonish picture of Wade, which everyone signed. Wade's surprise birthday cake was delivered with
song. It went over especially well; we managed not to set the
boat afire with the forest of flickering candles.

Wednesday December 6
1415 GMT
Position at 1200 GMT: 17° 05´ N, 59° 29´ W
Noon-to-noon distance: 196 nautical miles
Making 8 knots on a heading of 310° magnetic
Wind is from the northeast at about 15 knots

Walter Barnum's record holds.

Antigua now lies about 130 nautical miles to our west so we should arrive there in the wee hours of Thursday morning. We'll probably anchor in Falmouth Harbor, then see if there's a place at the Antigua Yacht Club Marina in Falmouth or Nelson's Dockyard in English Harbor. I've tried to reach English Harbor by SSB radio, with no success. I'll now email via Inmarsat.

The crew are very excited, sniffing for land air while they polish the brass. We regret only that everyone ashore will be asleep when we arrive in a party mood. Well, sail training is about self-restraint and discipline, is it not?

Thursday December 7
1301 GMT
Antigua Yacht Club Marina, Falmouth Harbor, Antigua

We arrived safely at 0910 GMT (0510 in Antigua). The approach was somewhat spooky because the moon had gone down. We enjoyed seeing the sun come up while at anchor in Falmouth Harbor.

Total nautical miles sailed from Tenerife: 3,205

Time underway: 16 days, 21 hours

Total amount of fuel used: 39 gallons, about four more than the crossing to England.

This is the peak of the annual Nicholson Yacht Charter Festival, so the Antigua Yacht Club Marina has only one available berth, which is so tight they want me to look at it before we try to maneuver into it. They're sending a boat for me, so we can avoid gymnastics of assembling our inflatable dinghy. I'll learn about dock rates and decide what we can afford. The crew are pressuring for us to clear customs; they're very keen to get ashore – a desire that I do not fully understand. For now, brass polishing and a major deck scrub are serving to distract the crew from their lust for shore.

MPG on Land and Sea
We used 35 gallons of diesel for charging batteries and refrigeration on the Halifax-to-Gosport run, which was just under 3,000 nautical miles. We used 39 gallons for the Canaries to Antigua leg of just over 3,200 nautical miles. Since 6,200 nautical miles equals 7,135 miles on land, fuel efficiency for the two transatlantic legs was about 96.4 miles per gallon!

... later December 7
2018 GMT

We're at the Antigua Yacht Club Marina, in a slip that's so snug you couldn't slide a piece of paper in alongside us. I am waiting to learn what special rate Carlo, the owner of both the marina and a classic yacht, will offer. I'll know then if we can afford to stay here. I know he'll be as generous as possible. For now it is very good that the crew can get to shore easily. If we had to rely on the dinghy, we'd need to set times for drop-offs and pick-ups.

The Nicholson Festival is an opportunity for Caribbean charter yachts to market their wares. Only those who are here to see it themselves would believe the size and extravagance of yachting's outer limits. There are mega-yachts all around us, colossal in scale. Two sloops here have masts that are taller than any other in the sloop world. These are taller than the 166-foot masts on J-boats, and measure 191 feet. Then there are motor yachts large enough to carry a 60-foot sailboat on deck.

We're just one of the classics which, curiously enough in this setting, attracts considerable attention. The warmth of wood and elegance of tradition still catch many eyes. We're docked next to a Herreshoff New York 40, *Vixen II*, the only other classic yacht at this marina. She was converted to a schooner more than 20 years ago and has had a rather dramatic hull rebuild. Her owner told me about a rigging disaster: the foremast lost a glue seam and exploded, to dangle from the mainmast. Glad we made it across without masts exploding.

The heat is extreme, 92° F in the shade – a great contrast to the shocking cold wave folks are enduring back in Connecticut. The crew are eating ashore tonight to give Lee a break.

Brilliant looks clean and neat. Her brass and varnish glimmer in the tropical sun. Any negative memories of this passage fade rapidly into cherished experience.

Captain George Moffett returned home to Connecticut on December 17 for a few weeks' vacation. Brilliant spent the winter in Antigua, resting for a while in the care of Maynard and Anne Bray, maritime historians, authors, and former Mystic Seaport staff. George returned to Antigua on January 26, 2001, to take Brilliant on charter cruises until late April.

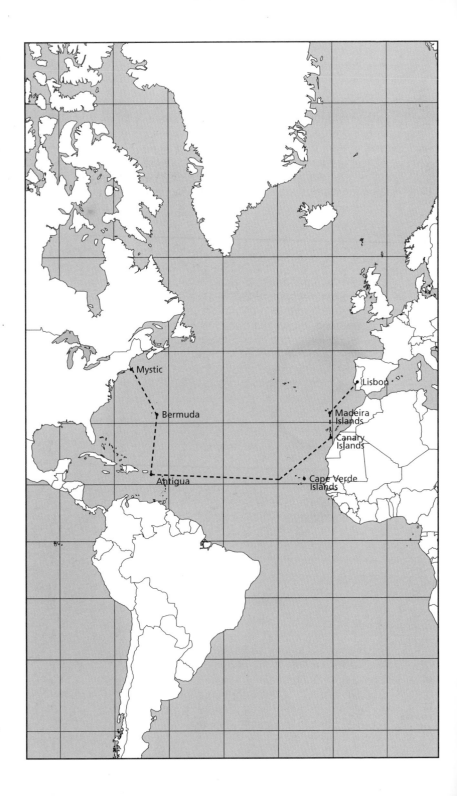

Chapter Four

Hard Journey Home
April 8 - May 19, 2001

After several months under charter, we set the pace in a vintage regatta ... maintain speed in a storm ... take shelter in Bermuda ... battle a Gulf Stream tempest ... and arrive safely home.

Sunday April 8, 2001
Falmouth Harbor, Antigua

In the upcoming regatta, we'll race in the "vintage class" with some of the world's great classic yachts including *Ticonderoga*, designed by L. Francis Herreshoff, and *Dione*, *Sincerity*, *Bella Aventure*, *Sumurun*, and *Latifa*, by the Scottish designer William Fife. Joel White's *White Wings* and *Wild Horses* are entered, as is Edson Schock's *Vileehi*. Sadly *Stormy Weather*, which, like *Brilliant*, was designed by Olin Stephens, will not be here. She has consistently shown her speed in this event and many others in the Caribbean circuit.

More than 45 boats are registered for the event. They range in size from a 200-foot, three-masted schooner named *Fleurtje*, to smaller vessels our size. *Endeavour* and *Whitehawk* are here among the big speedsters. My guess is that the boat to beat on corrected time will be *Latifa*, a famous 1936 Fife that was built for racing. Her very successful history includes winning line

111

Crew List
April 30 - May 9, 2001
Antigua - Bermuda

Professional Crew

George Moffett, captain
Ledyard, CT

Laurie Belisle, mate
Maynard, MA

Keith Chmura, cook
Sauquoit, NY

Cadets

Andy Baxter
Bigfork, MT

Jaime Brown
Grafton, MA

Francine Piersol
Westfield, NY

Walter Piersol
Westfield, NY

George Ichabod Rockwood, Jr.
Harwichport, MA

Sybil Smith
Boulder, CO

honors three times in the Fastnet Race. She's perfectly maintained, as are most of these vessels.

There are three days of races, consisting of three short courses of about 20 nautical miles just outside of Antigua's English and Falmouth Harbors. Usually there is good wind, typically 15 to 20 knots, with related seas and ocean swells.

Brilliant is looking good with a fresh coat of paint on the topsides and boot top. We've done our best to give her a good bottom finish. Varnishing is a struggle in this hot sun. To give you an idea, the rail cap just got its fifth coat since leaving Mystic last summer and we should do a sixth before heading north. We had two men up each mast varnishing to preserve the hard work of Amy Hagberg , who stripped them two years ago. There are people down here who make a very good living varnishing the mega-yachts that winter in the Caribbean. Some live in very large houses as a reward for their very hard work.

The Challenges of Chartering

All went well this first week of chartering, although there is a considerable learning curve in how to run the vessel as a charter and how to prepare food and drink to a standard that's above our norm as a sail training vessel.

High demand for ice and cooled drinks has stretched the limits of our space and systems. The refrigeration system started to show signs of failing, so I brought in a specialist who understands our type of system. At this moment, an evacuation pump is running to clear the unit of moisture in preparation for a recharge of refrigerant.

A special yacht provisioning service helps us with the meat, which is a difficult matter; we have a hard time keeping it fresh long enough, given our refrigerator systems.

A new, second inflatable arrives tomorrow (maybe), so we'll have two outboards and two dinghies to provide more flexibility for those who want to go snorkeling and those who do not.

Navigation has been a bit of a challenge; there are almost no buoys in most areas and navigation into the shallows is done by a combination of bearings, GPS, and visual recognition of reefs, which become different colors in various depths of water. This is a bit spooky, but it'll become less stressful with a couple more weeks' experience.

We're learning.

— Captain George Moffett

Sunday April 29
1607 EDT
Falmouth Harbor, Antigua

The charter season of February through April is behind us. A total of six one-week charters came to a grand close with the Antigua Classic Yacht Regatta. In three days of racing, *Brilliant* took two firsts and a second to place first in her class. She also received an award for "fastest elapsed time" among the schooners. Appropriately, *Brilliant* clinched first-in-class on April 23 – her 70th birthday!

Brilliant's speed was impressive. We made 9 knots most of the time and consistently led the fleet, with only J-class boats catching us before the finish. It's quite a thrill to lead 58 boats around the course!

Here's how fast we were: our class started second in the set of five fleets. The J-boats started 45 minutes after us, and it took three to four hours for them to catch us. In the third race, we crossed the finish line just seconds ahead of *Endeavour*; we could see the whites of her bowman's eyes! It was a high moment for us. None of the other big boats, young or old, could catch us. The two most challenging boats in our class were Herreshoffs: *Vixen II* and the very recently fully restored *Gallant*.

Laurie Belisle has joined *Brilliant* as mate and will stay on through late May. Laurie is very able. She is an experienced skipper with a 200-ton coastal master's license, soon to be upgraded to ocean class. Her sailing background includes working aboard high-end yachts and sail training aboard such vessels as *Tole Mour* and *Ernestina*.

Our new cook, Keith Chmura, will join us for the Antigua 2001 Classic Yacht Regatta at the end of this month, the return passages via Bermuda, and then on through the season to September. Keith is really more of a chef than a cook, used to gourmet cooking on fancy boats. He is coming to learn about sailing and seamanship, an opportunity for which he is willing to take a big pay cut. We'll have to be careful not to get fat in the meantime.

Laurie did a great job of managing the green crew. Two days of drills and three days of racing turned us into a smooth team. Keith, our cook, kept us well-fed and helped a great deal on deck when he wasn't busy in the galley.

Our departure from Antigua is set for noon tomorrow. Laurie, Keith, and I have been focused on preparing the boat over the past few days; we feel good about her readiness. As of this afternoon, our crew for the passage to Bermuda are aboard. We're already in the middle of safety drills and have discussed watch plans, weather issues, and general ship's operations. Tomorrow morning we'll continue with safety drills and take care of customs clearance, fuel up, various payments, and other operation details.

The latest weather report from the Navy predicts fair winds for at least the first few days. After that, we may run into difficult headwinds but it's too early to tell with confidence. We'll listen to amateur meteorologist Herb Hilgenberg's broadcast to gain more insight on the weather.

As the gull flies, the passage to Bermuda is about 950 nautical miles, but we'll sail farther than that unless we have a great deal of luck. Our goal is to reach Bermuda no later than May 9th. We'll be docked at the Royal Bermuda Yacht Club.

I'll try to continue the pattern of sending one email every day. We have a new IBM ThinkPad laptop up and running. Salt water killed our first laptop and did in our stationary computer as well. The IBM's record is pretty good, having traveled about 10,000 nautical miles with us through wild weather and calm. I'll be very careful to protect this unit because it's this or nothing.

The following entry marks the beginning of Brilliant's *journey home.*

Monday April 30
1949 EDT
Current position: 17° 31´ N, 62° 02´ W, with Bermuda 900 nautical
miles to the north
On a close-reach, making 9 knots on a heading of 005° magnetic
East winds at 15 to 20 knots, seas about three feet

I can't tell you how wonderful it is to be under way again with the prospect of days at sea, away from the many distractions and details that clutter the mind. We have a fine crew who have been thoroughly briefed on safety. We departed Antigua at 1410 local time.

Our biggest hurdle before leaving was that I had to finish the petty cash report for the month of April and send it off by Federal Express; it's the end of our fiscal year. I couldn't do this earlier because I had to wait for some large bills that were coming in today, such as dockage for the nearly four months since we arrived in Antigua December 7th! Carlo Franconi, the marina's owner, gave us a special deal at less than half the normal rate. Carlo owns a classic, 70-foot Fife called *Mariella*, and he loves to have other classics in his marina. We also had to pay the National Park Service for the use of Antiguan waters and shore facilities.

All things considered, we were under way in pretty good time. Now we're just southwest of Barbuda and darkness has set in with only a hint of the moon behind cloud cover. We know these perfect conditions will not last, but we're surely enjoying the ride for now.

Some seasickness has set in, as might be expected with the boat moving around so much. It would be much worse if we were headed just 15 degrees more to the east; we're lucky to have this relatively smooth reach.

Tuesday May 1
2035 EDT
Position at 1200 EDT: 19° 58' N, 62° 26' W
Position at 2000 EDT: 21° 05' N, 62° 31' W
Making 8 knots on a course of 015° magnetic

We logged 216 nautical miles in our first 24 hours, even with some fussing in setting the sails and escaping the clutter of the harbor! Much of the time we exceeded 9 knots with perfect 17- to 21-knot winds out of the east.

This is the same prevailing wind that carried centuries of trade, including countless slaves in misery. This breeze has made the cycle so many times that I'm sure the air we feel on our faces has known the skin of thousands before. We're feeling the size of the sea and sky.

In recent hours we've experienced an easing of the wind, now down to 11 to 16 knots, with a corresponding drop in our speed, even though we changed to a #1 jib. At first light tomorrow, we'll set the big reacher that carried us so faithfully across the Atlantic – virtually all of the 3,205 nautical miles from the Canaries to Antigua.

The crew are settling in, their initial seasickness almost forgotten. I felt a little uneasy in my own tummy earlier today; I moved too quickly from work below to a detailed repair on deck without first stopping to catch a breath of fresh air and a sight of clear horizon.

Some aboard have been with us before and are very welcome returns:

•Walter and Francine Piersol are longtime friends of *Brilliant* who have sailed four programs, including three Don Treworgy navigation weekends! Walt and Francine have built their own boat, are seasoned sailors and perfect shipmates.

• We have George Rockwood, also a boat owner, who sailed two of our weekend adult programs and comes with many thousands of miles of ocean experience. He has raced and cruised with most of the well-known sailors of the past four decades and has enormous depth of feel for the sea.

• Jaime Brown, our youngest crew member, begins her ocean sailing career with this sail. She'll return to her Cape Cod business with a growing restlessness for the sea; I feel rather sure of that. She has already spent hours at the helm in quartering, stern-kicking swells – conditions that are most frustrating for a helmsperson.

Also joining us for the first time are Sybil Smith from Colorado and Andy Baxter from Montana. Both have sailed before, Sybil extensively in smaller craft and Andy as a professional skipper some years ago. Andy was quick to the end of the bowsprit, while Sybil took the helm in tricky conditions during this evening's sail change. We're glad that the western

U.S. is represented with such enthusiasm to round out our high-spirited crew. All hands took part in setting the fisherman and changing jibs. Day two at sea suggests our crew will be ready for more difficult weather ahead.

Listening to a very broken message from Herb, we gather that there's a gale to our northwest in the Bahamas. We'll learn, perhaps in a day or two, if the system will flow east and meet us south of Bermuda or dissipate to our advantage. For now, we embrace the warmth of the moment, enjoying *Brilliant's* sea-kindly way of answering the swells with a gentle undulation.

Wednesday May 2
0626 EDT
Position at 0600 EDT: 22° 27′ N, 62° 31′ W

We're under heavy cloud cover and a very red sunrise, so we're wondering if we're already far enough north to experience some of that low I mentioned yesterday. Our most recent weather map suggests we shouldn't experience wind changes associated with the front until 25° N. We're now 18 nautical miles east of our rhumb line and having to steer 015° magnetic to keep her moving without slatting the sails. I'm hoping Don Treworgy will take a look at the map on the Navy's Web site and give me an idea when to expect trouble or significant wind shifts. We've had difficulty understanding Herb and haven't been able to receive weather faxes.

... later May 2
2207 EDT
Position at 1200 EDT: 23° 16′ N, 62° 23′ W
Current position: 24° 22′ N, 62° 13′ W
East-southeast winds, 17 to 21 knots, pushing us along for a 200-nautical-mile day

Late this afternoon everything changed, with a weather system that came in, dumped tons of water and shifted the wind to the south. This corresponds with part of the Navy weather forecast from Don, which predicted this to our west.

It moved east, however and caught us. We just recovered from a very heavy squall, for which we took the precaution of dropping all sails but the fore; the sky looked ominous in the moonlit grayness and even more so on radar. As it turned out, the winds were no more than 22 to 27 knots, but the rain could not have been more dense. We're motoring now as we go into a watch change. We'll set sail again when we have more hands on deck.

We just broke the 500-nautical-mile mark for Bermuda, so we're well ahead of schedule. It'll be interesting to see if the forecast is correct for tomorrow, when we hope for strong winds out of the east again.

Thursday May 3
0637 EDT
Current position: 25° 27´ N, 62°40´ W
Making 9 knots on a course of 000° magnetic

The updated Navy weather report explains perfectly the weather we've been experiencing since yesterday afternoon. Rain squalls, heavily overcast skies with occasional lightning in the distance, and a wind shift to the south; it's now west-southwest and filling in to 17 to 21 knots. We seem to be in the southern or southwest quadrant of the low. The wind may bend around to the northwest as we move up the west side of the low pressure center.

… later May 3
1420 EDT
Position at 1200 EDT: 26° 18´ N, 62° 50´ W
On a course of 055° magnetic
North-northwest winds at 15 knots

We seem to be on the northwest edge of the low's center because the wind has gone weak for us, while a vessel to our west-northwest is experiencing 25 knots out of the northeast. Herb Hilgenberg predicts a belt of 25- to 30-knot winds, with gusts up to 40 knots, in the area between 27° N and 30° N. So, we've shortened down to our heavy-weather #3 jib, but have only one reef in the main. We're actually motorsailing for now, because we're so shortened-down. We'll soon tack in anticipation of the northeaster. It looks like we'll have a bit of a slog for the next day or two, paying our dues for the bliss of the last few days.

It's hard to believe we are only 364 miles from Bermuda.

... still later May 3
1732 EDT
Current position: 26° 47′ N, 63° 00′ W
Making 7 to 8 knots on a heading of 330° magnetic – wishing for 000° magnetic!
Bermuda is 346 nautical miles to our north

All changed shortly after my last email. Indeed, we must have been virtually in the center of the low, because minutes after I said we were motorsailing, the wind freshened out of the northeast. We're now struggling with wind of about 30 knots. We put a second reef in the main but kept it furled because we already have enough power with the heavy-weather jib, forestaysail, and foresail. The seas are heavy, awkward, and steep. It's extremely wet on deck with white water rushing from fore to aft, soaking everyone in the cockpit. It's wild out here – we'll all be glad when this eases.

Friday May 4
1904 EDT
Position at 1200 EDT: 28° 55′ N, 64° 01′ W
Position at 1800 EDT: 29° 56′ N, 64° 17′ W

We're very happy – some of us more than others – to have the heavy weather behind us. Two of the crew have just emerged from their bunks after taking almost 24 hours refuge. The winds are now about 12 knots, having eased from 25 gusting to 30. We've decided to motorsail the remaining 162 nautical miles. It would be easiest to arrive in daylight, but we'll more likely make landfall in the darkness of early evening.

Herb forecasts light winds near Bermuda until a low recently generated over the Bahamas (near 27° N, 77° W) joins forces with another low that's south of us, creating what Herb thinks will be a tempest. He's advising mariners in this area to head for Bermuda and take shelter because this great merging of energy could happen as early as Sunday. If this proves true, we're lucky once again to have slipped through bad weather without a real pasting. Beating in 25- to 30-knot winds is quite enough.

Don's weather support has been crucial because I hadn't been able to receive weather faxes or hear Herb until this afternoon. Others in our area have been able to hear Herb clearly, so I think our receiver needs a check-up. I've been very meticulous about keeping this laptop well-protected from water, which has been in abundance everywhere, on deck and below, for the last 24 hours.

It's always fun to see the spirits of the crew rise as the seas lie down and the howling winds subside. Holding on for dear life, when every little move is a challenge, grows old quickly.

Earlier this afternoon we leapt off a wave and crashed into the trough with such violence that the whole ship shuddered like I've never felt before. I felt bad for the old girl, and somewhat guilty for putting her to such a test at her advanced age. But I think *Brilliant* is like other 70-year-olds who, blessed with strength and health, love to work hard and play hard. She is by no means ready for the rocking chair. Like many others who have sailed *Brilliant*, we'll know retirement before she does.

We've just gone through a watch change after another of Keith's fine dinners. For the off-watch, a warm, somewhat stationary bunk is very appealing indeed as we begin our last full night at sea.

Saturday May 5
1252 EDT
Position at 1200 EDT: 32° 05′ N, 64° 33′ W, about 13 nautical miles southeast of Bermuda
Motorsailing in very light east-southeast winds, making just under 8 knots

There is an increasing probability of strong winds Sunday and possibly a gale on Monday, so we're very glad to have made a fast passage. Unless our motor fails in the next couple of hours, we'll have made the passage in five days plus a few minutes.

Magic Carpet, a Sparkman & Stephens yawl that sailed in the Antigua Classic Yacht Regatta and was next to us at the marina, is about 150 nautical miles to our southwest. She intended to sail straight to Newport, RI, but may duck in to Bermuda to avoid a gale. The winds may begin to build tomorrow, so I hope they can reach Bermuda before a beast emerges.

All hands look forward to showers and some real rest. Tonight we'll stay in St. George's harbor, where we have to clear customs. We'll move on to Hamilton tomorrow, where the Royal Bermuda Yacht Club has reserved a place for us.

... later May 5
1546 EDT

Brilliant was secured to the customs dock in St. George's an hour ago. All's well.

Monday May 7
1206 EDT
Hamilton, Bermuda

We were very happy to be secured to the Royal Bermuda Yacht Club dock yesterday, after motoring for two hours from St. George's to Hamilton. We felt the wind building through the afternoon; it started a mournful cry in the rigging during the night. The storm system is expected to intensify further today, with winds reaching 35 knots and seas building to 15 to 18 feet.

Had the seas been much larger than 5 feet from the northeast yesterday, we wouldn't have been able to leave St. George's. The narrow exit faces east and one must motor out because there is no room to tack. With our engine at full throttle, we could only make 3 knots into the head seas as we exited the narrows. Once again we were lucky to have good timing with the weather.

Boats at sea south of here are working hard with discontented crews. Dismastings are being reported; the most recent incident happened 160 nautical miles northwest of Bermuda.

Thinking about the passage from Antigua and looking closely at the numbers, we realized that it was quite a remarkable sail. Dock to dock, we logged 986 nautical miles in five days and 35 minutes. If we subtract the distance and time we spent milling around setting sail and waiting for a place to dock in St. George's, we really did 985 nautical miles in five days – very close to an average of 200 nautical miles a day for the entire passage!

While we sailed close-hauled in 25- to 30-knot winds, other boats in the area were having trouble. One was dismasted and another suffered four knockdowns. A classic 1912 Fife 60-foot schooner named *Elisa* blew out her foresail. *Magic Carpet* shortened down to storm trysail and a staysail. *Kisses*, a new 175-foot Feadship, took a beating and slowed down to 3.5 knots. *Brilliant* maintained 8 knots, most of the time without a mainsail. Later she sailed even better, without being over-pressed, once we set the double-reefed main. She is truly a very good sea boat.

Laurie, the mate, has sailed on large modern yachts and says none of them would have done as well in the same conditions. All would have been even more uncomfortable, with extreme pounding. When sailing offshore, there is much to be said for a long keel, heavy displacement, a good measure of lead, a low-aspect rig and a brave bowsprit-climbing, reef-tucking crew.

There have been no complaints about arriving early. The day in St. George's gave us a chance to free the brass from a cover of saltwater-induced tarnish, to air clothing, rediscover lost items, and rest. (Well, some of us rested.) Today we'll do a little more cleaning, then go ashore for relaxed exploration of the island – all of this, after a late breakfast. Some of the young and foolish, or older and ill-advised, stayed out late last night – something beyond my comprehension as I contemplated the inside of my eyelids.

Here are some words from Laurie Belisle:

"We did heave sighs of relief as we tossed the first dock lines, glad to have arrived before winds and seas built up.

"Shipboard life is very organized in its demands: the time to eat, stand watch, sleep, and clean are all set – with little variance. I'm now a bit at odds, trying to decide what my priorities will be ashore: telephone, email, shower (my first hot one in four months!), sleep, or drink? Bermuda is at a crossroads for many yachts going north or to Europe, so it's always a good place to meet friends I haven't seen in months.

"Our crew is impressed by Front Street and its ample opportunities for jewel shopping. Two cruise ships that dwarf the buildings at shoreside arrived this morning, supplying the merchants with 4,000 shoppers!"

... later May 7
1626 EDT

Bermuda Harbor Radio now reports steady winds at 34 knots gusting to 44; the forecast has been changed to winds of 25 to 40 knots and seas to 20 feet! Gads, we are happy to be on the lee side of the dock. Yesterday the dock attendant wanted to put us on the weather side. I said, "Don't you think, with a gale tomorrow out of the northeast, it would be better on the lee side?" He agreed and was willing to move two boats to make it possible. That was very generous and accommodating; we're very grateful to the Yacht Club for such hospitality. Both Laurie and I were greatly relieved. We know how miserable we'd be if we were on the weather side. It's really blowing!

Wednesday May 9
1126 EDT
Hamilton, Bermuda

It rained heavily yesterday and through the night. At this time, some clear sky is beginning to show. Yesterday afternoon, Bermuda Harbor Radio recorded steady wind between 35 and 45 knots with gusts to 53! We know of a passenger plane that did not land yesterday morning because of crosswinds. Two big cruise ships did not depart on schedule, so two others had to hold station outside of Bermuda. You can be sure those passengers were not happy.

When we raced to England in July, we had a gale that was similar in strength, with winds steady at 35 knots, gusting to 48. We had *Brilliant* shortened down to storm trysail and forestaysail and made a steady 8 to 9 knots on a beam- to close-reach. Some boats in that race hove to during the gale for fear of losing their rigs from the pitching. It's a tribute to *Brilliant's* strength that she carried on with such speed, and it's a reminder of Olin and Rod's belief that strength is the single most important characteristic for an ocean sailing boat. *Brilliant's* strength aside, I'm very glad we weren't trying to reach Bermuda in the conditions of the past few days.

The crew are ashore for now; all but one passenger have left for hotel rooms. The boat is very quiet. It's strange, but somehow welcome, to hear no voices.

We had a good visit with Joe Postich and Wendy Bliss, a couple who are restoring the classic yacht *Chicane* in the Royal Naval Shipyard. The time is coming for the classic-boat magazines to address this high-quality restoration, which is now in its ninth year. Despite taking the time to show their project to some 14,000 visitors, Joe and Wendy have maintained extraordinary focus on the exacting details. They showed the seven of us around with grace and elegance. *Chicane* should be invited to visit schools that teach wooden-boat building and restoration, to inspire students and teachers with her example of perfection.

Friday May 11
1419 EDT
Hamilton, Bermuda

It looks like high pressure will dominate the early part of the upcoming final leg of our trip. But I've made note of a serious cold front that is marching across the eastern U.S. and coming our way. It will be interesting to see if this cold front weakens or strengthens.

Sunday May 13
0904 EDT
Hamilton, Bermuda

Our six passengers, all men, have arrived on the island and will join us early this afternoon with the prospect of motoring over to St. George's today. Five have sailed with us before; all understand the nature of this potentially challenging passage. We'll clear customs tomorrow morning and make a last minute decision about our departure.

The weather is looking good, except for a cold front that will pass this area Monday evening. It's the same front that must have just passed over New England. I heard that it was strong over land. I'm not sure if we'll have enough information

---

Crew List
May 13 - May 19
Bermuda - Mystic Seaport, Connecticut

Professional Crew

George Moffett, captain
Ledyard, CT

Laurie Belisle, mate
Maynard, MA

Keith Chmura, cook
Sauquoit, NY

Cadets

John Fred Grunigen
Ashford, CT

Donald George Hunsicker
Canton, MA

George Ichabod Rockwood, Jr.
Harwichport, MA

David Charles Sabourin
Germantown, MD

Gary Foster Stephens
Pomfret Center, CT

Andrew Jay Vomastek
Chester, CT

Monday morning to know how strong it'll be when it reaches this area. The wind is expected to be west before the front and veer northwest after, which would put it on our nose at 15 to 20 knots. However, it's forecast to back to the west again as the system moves further east. If we hear that the front is nearby and nasty, we may delay departure to Tuesday. Or we may leave later today. We hope that the wind will back to the southwest eventually. If it doesn't, we'll have a very slow passage.

The last two times that *Brilliant* returned from Bermuda to Mystic, in 1985 and in 1994, strong winds enabled us to do the trip in less than four days. *Brilliant* also visited Bermuda in 1932, 1936, and 1946 for races.

Brian Billings, former commodore of the Royal Bermuda Yacht Club, took us on a grand harbor tour yesterday afternoon. We saw many of the small islands, reefs, and coves that make Bermuda such a wonder of nature. The economy is strong here, evidenced by a great amount of new construction – corporate structures as well as waterfront homes.

Mystic Seaport's very dedicated trustee Bill Ridgway stopped by yesterday with his wife Carole. We appreciated the enthusiasm he showed for *Brilliant* and her excellent condition after the last lively 11,000 nautical miles. We're pulling out the last of our $3,000 worth of charts that another trustee, Frank Bohlen, so carefully compiled before our departure. This was an enormous task; I'm grateful to Frank for taking this task off my hands at a time when so much was spinning in my head. Even in this electronic age, we still need paper charts aboard, not to mention other, traditional navigation tools for backup. For example, *Brilliant's* original 1932 taffrail log still lives aboard, ready to serve should a lightning bolt clean out all of the modern "magic boxes."

... later May 13
1607 EDT

Based on the latest weather forecast, which predicts winds from the northwest tomorrow, we've left Bermuda, after clearing customs and fueling. Our departure time was 1535 EDT.

Memorial at Sea

On Sunday May 13, *Brilliant* slowed to a near crawl about 50 nautical miles from Bermuda, at 33° 02' N, 65° 12' W. Her crew paused for a moment of silence at 2200 EDT and placed flowers on the water in memory of Susan Howell and Andrea Lee, two friends of Mystic Seaport, who were lost at sea with 17 others when the *Marques* sank in 1984. Susan was Associate Planetarium Director at Mystic Seaport, a navigation instructor, and author of the book, *Practical Celestial Navigation*.

Monday May 14
0736 EDT
Current position: 34° 04′ N, 66° 17′ W; about 508 nautical miles from Watch Hill, RI

We left Bermuda a little earlier than intended because we were concerned about the weather forecast, which said that the winds would probably go northwest today. There was a good breeze blowing yesterday out of the west-southwest, so we figured we should make headway while we could. We were abeam of Kitchen Shoals at the northwest corner of the Bermuda reef at 1630 EDT and made good speed through the late afternoon and night. We're only 125 miles closer to Mystic, but that will be a welcome head start if the wind goes northwest.

The boat moved around a lot last night and with a crew that's new to the vessel, no one slept. Today, exhaustion shows on everyone's face.

A line of squalls rushed through this morning at the change of watch, so we shortened sail and carried through it nicely. Now we need to reset sail to keep her moving through choppy post-frontal seas and lighter air – but with only one watch on deck, we're short-handed. We want the off-watch to get some rest, so we're motorsailing in a perfectly good breeze.

Laurie and I have not slept at all and feel like we could sleep standing up. That's really the way everyone feels. Keith did a heroic job of preparing dinner and breakfast in a wildly leaping galley.

Some unusual local currents must have helped us along last night because we had sustained periods of speed greater

than 10 knots, according to the GPS. Our watch saw many
10.4s and several 10.7s – not normal speeds for *Brilliant*. We've
heard that there are odd currents around Bermuda. We are
working ourselves west of the course to Watch Hill (343° magnetic) to stay clear of a southeast-flowing meander in the Gulf
Stream, which must be kept to our east if possible. We also
want to be a bit to the west in anticipation of the wind veering northwest.

... later May 14
1643 EDT
Position at 1200 EDT: 34° 36′ N, 66° 32′ W
Position at 1800 EDT: 35° 05′ N, 66° 45′ W

We have a four-day-old satellite image that seems to show
a meander in the Gulf Stream. The meander's upper bend
starts in a southeast direction on the south wall at 37.5° N,
69.5° W. The lower bend, where the south wall returns to the
northeast is at 36.5° N, 66.5° W.

It looks like we'll have northwest winds for a while at 25
to 30 knots. We're having a pretty hard go of it. The seas are
rather lumpy and very uncomfortable.

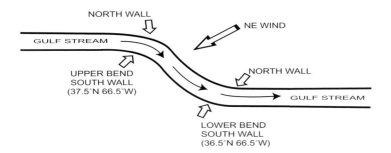

... still later May 14
1824 EDT

We've tacked to sail west, thinking it would be a bad idea
to cross the Gulf Stream north of here because of the meander

and because northeasterly winds are predicted for this area. With strong winds blowing against the Gulf Stream current, the seas will certainly be extremely rough. We'll have to sail about a hundred miles west to get around the meander, but the alternative isn't acceptable, given our already exhausted state.

We're sailing very slowly to minimize the action and let people move around safely and get some rest. I'm very worried that someone could be injured due to exhaustion and a misstep or loss of balance.

... later yet May 14
2017 EDT

We are about to be overtaken from the north by a very nasty-looking front with tall black clouds and lots of lightning. It's the third front today, but looks to be the most threatening by far. If you don't hear from us tomorrow, it may be because all systems are down in the electrical storm. I send this only to reduce worry and because this looks like a pretty serious set of weather. I'm unplugging as many gadgets as possible.

Tuesday May 15
0821 EDT
Current position: 35° 35´ N, 67° 18´ W
Making 4.5 knots on a heading of 280° magnetic

We've been through several severe fronts with winds of more than 40 knots, rain, sleet, and lots of lightning – very intense. In anticipation of a possible gale, we've shortened down to storm trysail, fore, and forestaysail. We're just jogging along, as we have been for more than 24 hours, so nobody gets hurt. With all of the squalls around us, we kept the main down all night.

I'm concerned about how long it'll take to get through the southwest quadrant of this big low, especially since it's almost certain that we'll enter the Gulf Stream in a gale or a northeaster. After the latest strong cold front roared through, the wind became unsteady – sometimes gusting above 20 knots;

sometimes almost calm. Up and down; up and down: It's hard to keep the boat moving.

We've had some equipment failures to remind us how lucky we've been. The jib halyard lost a shackle aloft and came down with the jib. The midship head broke today. The galley stove lost some parts. Gads, the interior of the boat looks a frightful mess with gear everywhere and crew on various bunks.

... later May 15
1531 EDT
Position at 1200 EDT: 35° 33´ N, 67° 38´ W
Motoring north-northwest on a course of 320° magnetic
The barometric pressure is falling slowly

We're not experiencing the weather that was forecast. Instead we have a near calm, with swells and lumps left over from the various fronts and squalls. One more squall front ran through an hour ago, but without high winds or electrical excitement. All is different from what we anticipated. I assume the blow will come, so we're motoring with just a bit of canvas set in this light northwester. There's a bear out there somewhere and we don't want to be surprised when we find it.

There's temptation to set lots of canvas, just to keep way on in these residual seas. We'd certainly have to do that if we were racing. However, we're all feeling a little gun shy. Perhaps it's a healthy loss of nerve to keep us from joining the optimists at the bottom of the ocean.

Both Laurie and I had night watches with dramatic weather so we and the entire crew are very happy to have the boat remain underfoot for awhile. We're pushing north to approach the Gulf Stream and still wondering if we'll get the northeaster tonight – just in time to kick up the Gulf Stream and welcome us in style. We'll keep this gale canvas set until we know more.

Keith continues to feed us well and is really a trooper in the wet and slippery galley. A leaky washboard on the forward hatch allows the white water on deck to find its way below, to the cook's feet. It's a problem we need to resolve, along with the problem of the midship head. I haven't found the courage yet to take the head apart. When the time comes it'll be my job because I know how these units look inside ... mechanically, I mean! The heads haven't been rebuilt since Joe Birkle volunteered and did such a heroic job in our workshop last spring.

The broken jib halyard wasn't a big issue because we have an alternative halyard, which enabled us to rehoist the sail as soon as it came down. It seems an unnecessary risk to go aloft to fix the primary halyard. If the forecast is correct, we may not need a jib for several days, anyway. The stove is working fine.

Quiet seas and the steady drone of the engine have given everyone a good rest; spirits have come to life again. Everyone seems to be taking the recent hardship with grim determination, although conversations have turned to the question of why people do this for recreation.

Don Hunsicker has actually had the presence of mind to take a few sights and start working them up with his own *Nautical Almanac* and H.O. 249 sight reduction tables. Hunsicker is another of Don Treworgy's incredibly devoted students.

Wednesday May 16
0803 EDT
Position at 0730 EDT: 36° 44´ N, 68° 11´ W; 335 nautical miles from Mystic
Making 6 knots on a course of 040° magnetic

That was a night to remember! The bear has arrived. Numerous squalls passed through in the darkness of the night. We had winds up to 50 knots, driving rain, exploding lightning, and white water raging everywhere. These were black watches for all.

Laurie says she'd never been so glad to have small sails up. She really had some wild ones. The storm trysail sheet became a piano wire and the forestaysail's leach buzzed with protest. The rail went under and the off-watch struggled to stay in our bunks. Keith's quarter berth is soaked so he took a berth in the diving fo'c'sle, only to learn he had to tack bunks with each tack of the ship, to keep from falling out. That weary, unrested look is back on each and every face.

What a bad place to be. I was sure we'd lose our communications to a burst of electrons from above. Some of these squall clouds glow at the bottom before the lightning rips a gap, joining positive to negative in its moment of fury. That glow must be a buildup of electrostatic charge just before the release of the lightning bolt. It's such an ominous sight, that strange green light under a flash-outlined cloud.

With dawn came a change of watch – very welcome for those above deck. Dave, Don, and Andy are on watch with Laurie, and George Rockwood, Gary, and John with me.

We must be nuts to be here. If you want a vacation that includes near-death anxieties, sailing in a small boat near the Gulf Stream is where you want to be. George Rockwood has done a lot of ocean racing, including races to Bermuda, and he is very grateful that this is not a race. We'd be flopping about in the chop between squalls, with too little wind to drive the boat unless we'd set miles of canvas, which would be taken in with great panic each time we were blasted with wind, rain, and electrons. We're glad we have the option of motoring under shortened sails.

Our strategy for crossing the Gulf Stream has changed dramatically. We'll enter the stream in the meander today and accept the setback to the southeast. We prefer this to delaying our entry until tomorrow. Delaying would put us farther west and in a better place to cross, but we'd be more likely to have a northeaster at the same time. It's better to cross the stream in a wind-with-tide situation, before the wind veers to the northeast. We'll be driven to the east by the current, and that'll be a heavy loss. But a northeast wind later would compensate by potentially enabling some westing in our course toward Mystic.

This plan assumes that the forecast is accurate. Herb Hilgenberg has advised vessels in the area to push west of 68° W longitude, which we have done. But now we must accept some easting to cross the Gulf Stream meander, which we think is about 30 nautical miles to our north.

... later May 16

2248 EDT
Position at 1030 EDT: 36° 56′ N, 68° 17′ W
Position at 1200 EDT: 37° 02′ N, 68° 24′ W
Position at 2235 EDT: 37° 36′ N, 69° 25′ W

We are not happy. That forecast strong northeaster caught us as we entered the meander of the Gulf Stream. Imprecise weather analysis, particularly in predicting the arrival times of large and small weather systems, is an ongoing problem.

Our thoughts quickly shifted from prediction to endurance: the major wind shift working against the tide created short, steep waves. *Brilliant* responded in a very disconcerting manner, falling off the waves and slamming on her side. Between slams, the boat was jerked in every direction. The crew's locomotion degenerated to a pathetic, wide-spread crawl on all fours. These seas make fools of us. Six hours of rough sailing helped us all understand why it's a bad idea to be in the Gulf Stream in a northeaster.

Naturally just before the wind arrived, my impatience with our under-canvassed waiting game reached its threshold and became unbearable. We had just finished bending on and hoisting the #3 jib when we noticed a sudden shift of the light breeze to the north-northeast. Hmmm, we said. Within minutes, the strong wind spoke to us in the rigging.

As Laurie and her watch began their long afternoon stretch, she was delighted to experience yet another energetic squall. This one had mere gusts of 35 to 40 knots, and just a few tons of rain, instead of oceans of it. She was even more pleased to find that I had insisted on setting an additional jib. Nothing broke, and we skimmed along for a few wild minutes before the seas went into chaos. Very soon all got better, settling down to a steady squall with less than 25- to 30-knot winds – quite ho-hum.

Laurie insists there's a conspiracy, because her watch always gets the worst weather. It's true, she has consistently received the worst, with a choice selection of squalls. She'd like to have a chat with whomever delivers the weather, especially on the topic of timing. She doesn't understand where or when she has offended. This has become a pretty big topic for crew discussion. Personally, I have no objections and will con-

tinue to accept my allocation of misery while showing great
respect for the judgment of whomever is in charge.

Naturally, when my watch came on at 6 P.M., the situation
greatly eased and the seas took on more friendly, understand-
able patterns. The ship's motion became more conducive to
walking upright with a semblance of dignity. Once again, we
cheerfully sent the previous watch (who had become delirious
shadows of their former selves) off to retirement. It has been
said that our comeuppance is at hand.

Some things did get fixed today while the other watch
played with squalls. You remember that broken head? It took
three hours to dismantle it completely; with a full kit of spare
parts on hand, we rebuilt the thing. It's probably not the first
time a head has been rebuilt at sea in a near gale, with parts
frequently airborne.

John worked with me on the reassembly. His strong hands
held the heavy parts while I tried to manipulate elements suit-
ed for the fingers of a dental surgeon. John's engineering background came in handy as we developed fresh approaches to
reassembly. When it was finally time to bolt the unit down,
Keith came to my rescue. I was having trouble holding the
heavy bowl in place so I could secure it to the bronze base. A
whiz at juggling dangerous objects, Keith was the right man
for the job. Our pride soared as we gazed on our fine work.
Keith then returned to the galley, that wonderland of mysteri-
ous leaks, where miracles are performed.

[Note from Don Treworgy: It could be said that *Brilliant's* chef
found his way to the galley through the head start program.]

Brilliant covered about 80 nautical miles in 15 hours on
May 16, bringing her 395 nautical miles from Bermuda with
about 255 nautical miles to go. Her speed made good was close
to 5.3 knots on a course of 316° true.

Sometimes, Trouble Comes in Waves …

0803 EDT, May 16
As if we didn't have enough to worry about, the engine tried to stop in the middle of the night. It cooperated when we changed the fuel filter. I'm suspicious about the quality of the fuel we've taken on in some of these remote stations. We're out of filters now; let's hope this problem won't revisit before we toss our lines to the dock at Mystic Seaport.

0844 EDT
The electrical inverter that runs the laptop charger is down and the 12-volt cigarette lighter adapter-charger that I used for the old laptop doesn't fit this one. I'm now down to the laptop battery itself, which is at 38 percent of capacity. I may be able to send one more message before the battery goes dead.

0948 EDT
I've rewired a new plug to the old cigarette lighter adapter. Perhaps it'll work for the laptop. The new unit calls for 16 volts and the old unit produces 19, so I may fry the battery and/or the computer itself with this old charger. If you do not hear from me again, I fried it.

The engine has started acting up again with pulsating losses of power, the same as before the last filter change. I'm feeling more certain that we got dirty fuel in Bermuda; it's loading up the filters fast. With no more filters on board, this is a problem.

Thursday May 17
0445 EDT
Current position: 37° 59´ N, 69° 40´ W; about 222 nautical miles from Watch Hill, RI

The most recent weather forecast sounds good, though perhaps there won't be enough wind to sail the rest of the trip. We think we are near the north wall of the Gulf Stream. The wind has gone weak out of the northeast, and we're thinking about motorsailing to get out of this last bit of the Gulf Stream.

... and solutions come in time

1040 EDT, May 16
All's well with the computer charging system, at least for the present. The plug conversion worked; the unit seems to tolerate the 19 volts from the old adapter charger.

0445 EDT, May 17
The engine continues to sputter and pulsate but it is running. I gave it another think to find a theory other than dirty fuel and clogged filters. I've seen dirtier filters with the engine still running. So I listened for a long time to the rhythm of changing rpms and noticed that the engine stalled when the boat pitched in the steep seas. It occurred to me that water in the exhaust pipe could be sloshing fore-and-aft, creating backpressure when it rushed into the silencers. The engine has an air supply blower that is very sensitive to backpressure. Even under the best of circumstances, we generate an awful lot of pressure because the boat has a very long exhaust pipe and two silencers in line.

For example, when there's too much water in the exhaust line, the engine won't start, especially in cooler weather. The engine starts right away if you drain the water from the line. Even a dirty air intake filter affects the starting of the engine.

Sure enough, when the sea state calmed a bit and I cleaned the air intake filter, the engine ran smoothly. We don't often motorsail in heavy seas under shortened canvas; the unusual pitching motion is what caused our problem. Perhaps cleaning the filter helped too. So it seems the fuel filter emergency has passed.

We've learned yet another new thing about this boat by operating her in new circumstances. We should look into one of the dry exhaust systems that are becoming increasingly popular. They have a good track record.

...later May 17
1427 EDT
Position at 1200 EDT: 38° 28′ N, 70° 16′ W
Close-hauled on a course of 352° magnetic
Winds at 20 to 25 knots, with seas in proportion

The Gulf Stream's influence lasted longer than we expected, extending well north of the reported north wall. But now we feel confident its effects are behind us; the boat isn't being pulled far from the course that we steer, and our hull speed through the water is close to our speed over the bottom, according to the GPS. This is our first sunny day since we left Bermuda and spirits are high.

My watch was just commenting that we've been close-hauled almost every day since leaving Bermuda. The only exception was our first day out, when we made a fast reach in anticipation of the coming northerly winds. This morning we finally took in the storm trysail and set the double-reefed main so the boat would move nicely without too much speed, enabling us to sail close-hauled in these seas.

All systems are working! The engine problem seems related to backpressure from water sloshing forward and aft in the long exhaust run, not filters and dirty fuel as we originally thought. [see sidebar on page 138]

We're 170 nautical miles southeast of Watch Hill. If we could sustain this speed and heading (which is very unlikely), we'd be anchoring someplace in Fishers Island Sound late Friday. That would give us some time to really clean the boat and ourselves, and get a good rest. Right now we look like cave dwellers – a terrible fright to the civilized – living in the drifting apparel of owners who are too tired to identify their own underwear. It's a good thing we all have an understanding.

...still later May 17
1925 EDT
Current position: 39° 10´ N, 70° 47´ W

I feel sure we'll be in Fishers Island Sound by late Friday afternoon. We started motorsailing just minutes ago. We're not pitching, so the engine sounds good. The seas have settled and it's almost calm. Watch Hill is now about 137 nautical miles ahead.

It seems hard to believe we're almost home.

Friday May 18
0110 EDT
Current position: 39° 42´ N, 71° 09´ W; about 100 miles south of Watch Hill
Making 6.5 knots under power on a course of 000° magnetic

I plan to make the 3:15 pm drawbridge on Mystic River tomorrow. This really works out well for us because it'll give us time to rest and to clean the boat, which is rather a mess. It'll take us many hours to polish the brass, clean, and reorganize. The group we have aboard will be delighted to pitch in and get on with a proper cleanup; they're keen to have *Brilliant* looking good for her return.

Postscript   Friday May 18

Brilliant came safely to dock at Noank (CT) Shipyard last night at about 6 P.M. After clearing customs, the crew received a joyous welcome from a few visitors. Among them was Olin Stephens, *Brilliant's* designer, who in his 90s is perhaps as resilient as his creation. He is certainly better travelled, having logged many more miles than *Brilliant's* 10,000 this year in his activities promoting yachting, as well as his autobiography, *All This and Sailing, Too* (Mystic Seaport, 2000, ISBN 0-913372-89-7).

Warm showers, provided by Noank Shipyard, made the crew feel like humans once again. And after a night's rest, the captain and crew gave *Brilliant* the tender loving care she deserved.

She looked brilliant indeed, when a small flotilla escorted her up the Mystic River to her own, familiar dock at Scott's Wharf, Mystic Seaport. She was welcomed home by Jim English, Acting President of Mystic Seaport, who led the assembled crowd in three cheers for *Brilliant* and three cheers for Captain George Moffett.

It had been 312 days since *Brilliant* left her dock the previous July.

Brilliant's crew parade in style and comfort to the awards ceremony in Halifax.

Hundreds of thousands of spectators line the shore in Halifax.
Katie Oman (left) and Miles Thurlow.

Ships from Classes A and B
jockey for position at the start
of the Halifax-to-Isle of Wight
Race.
Photo:
Jonathan Dickinson,
courtesy of ASTA

"... a spectacle none of us will ever forget: 18 tall ships, all in one spot, under full sail."

Brilliant's start from
Halifax. By nightfall,
she had overtaken the
boats seen here on
the horizon.
Photo:
Jonathan Dickinson,
courtesy of ASTA

Kruzenshtern, the world's second-largest tall ship, and eventual second-place winner overall, as seen from the deck of *Brilliant*, the eventual first-place winner overall.

Lee Wacker and Jon Feins on watch.

New London-to-Amsterdam crew:
Back row: Dan Parke, Christine Alberi, Frank Bohlen
Middle Row: Matt Lincoln, George Moffett, Lee Wacker
Front Row: Katie Oman, Chris Schmiedeskamp, Miles Thurlow, Jon Feins

A sunny day + dry clothes = happy crew

Laundry room with a view!

Celebrating the (approximate) halfway mark.

Katie Oman and Lee Wacker washing hair.

Katie Oman wipes down below.

Parading up the North Sea Canal to Amsterdam. Captain George Moffett (left), Katie Oman, Mate Christine Alberi.

Greeted by millions in Amsterdam.

In Amsterdam, "there are enough boats everywhere to walk from deck to deck."

The proud crew in Amsterdam:
Back Row: Katie Oman, Dan Parke, Jon Feins, Myles Thurlow, Chris Schmiedeskamp
Front Row: Lee Wacker, George Moffett, Christine Alberi, Frank Bohlen
Missing: Matthew Lincoln

Amsterdam-to-Gosport crew: Back Row: George Moffett, Brian Tabor, Katrina Yeager, Lee Wacker, Christine Alberi   Front Row: Jocelyn Jensen, Corey Brown, Florence Renault, Mary K. Bercaw Edwards, Sarah Fisher

Docked in one of Normandy's most beautiful harbors: Honfleur.

"Locking through" with the traditional fishing boats converted to passenger trade, France.

"*Brilliant* virtually glowed with a multitude of small boats in the background." (Dieppe)

A 1932 photo of the cabin, which looks the same today.
Photo: Morris Rosenfeld (© Mystic Seaport, Rosenfeld Collection)

Lee Wacker enjoys a rare
quiet moment in the cabin.
Photo: Rich King

"Any sail on deck must be lashed down securely, otherwise the seas could take charge."
Photo: Rich King

Tom Cunliffe does his thing. (Gosport to Kinsale)

Hannah Cunliffe does hers. (Gosport to Kinsale to Lisbon)

Christine reading on deck.   Photo: Rich King

Mate Christine Alberi (right), who also served as ship's photographer, in a rare moment before the camera. With her is Brittan Weinzierl. (Cascais to Canary Islands)

Madeira's landscape"...: a brutal jaggedness and forbidding presence makes the extent of settlement over the centuries seem astonishing."

Stark volcanic beauty: Tenerife, Canary Islands

Canary Islands-to-Antigua crew:
Back Row: David Thomas, George Moffett, Alyssa Stover, Wade Smith, Dan Bregman
Front Row: Christine Alberi, Cipperly Good, Lee Wacker, Rich King, Hamilton Moore

Drying sails in
Tenerife.

Downwind to Antigua, with preventers and vang in place.

Speeding along to Antigua.
Photo: Rich King

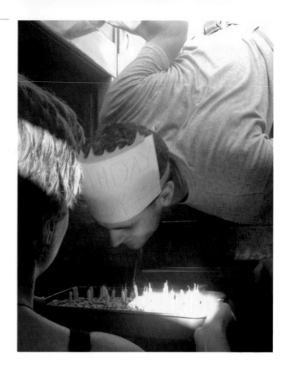

Celebrating Wade Smith's
28th birthday.

Among the Atlantic swells off Antigua.
Photo: Charlotte Hooijdonk

Pilgrims and Natives in dinner dress.
Photo: Rich King

Perhaps the happiest moment of all! Lee Wacker and Rich King with a mahimahi.

Cipperly Good achieves a goal: "Now I can steer *Brilliant* even with the compass covered."
Photo: Rich King

The reacher and the golliwobbler pull mightily.
Photo: Rich King

Rich King gets a better perspective on the world.

In Antigua: "I thought for sure Brilliant would be showing her seams, but she looks like she just left the dock at Mystic Seaport."

Antigua-to-Bermuda crew:
Left to right: Sybil Smith, Walter Piersol, Francine Piersol, Jaime Brown, Andy Baxter,
Laurie Belisle, Keith Chmura, George Moffett Missing: George Rockwell
Photo: George Rockwell

Homeward-bound with a double reef.
Photo: Walter Piersol

Moffett (center) with two of *Brilliant*'s former skippers (from 1953 on): Francis "Biff" Bowker (left) and Adrian Lane (right), 1983.
Photo: Mary Anne Stets

Brilliant under sail.
Photo: Mary Anne Stets

Appendices

Tall Ships® Racing Vessel Classes

A "tall ship" isn't necessarily one of the great square-riggers; any vessel in which at least half the people on board are aged between 15 and 25 and which is over 30 feet long at the waterline can enter American Sail Training Association or International Sail Training Association races.

For racing purposes, vessels taking part in a race are divided into classes and in some case, divisions within classes.

Description Of Classes

• Class A

    All square-rigged vessels over 120 feet (36.6 meters) length overall (LOA). Fore-and-aft-rigged vessels of 160 feet (48.8 meters) LOA and over.
    Square-rigged vessels include: ships, barks, barquentines, brigs, and brigantines.

• Division AII

    All square-rigged vessels with an LOA less than 120 feet (36.6 meters).

• Class B

    Fore-and-aft-rigged vessels between 100 feet (30.5 meters) and 160 feet (48.8 meters) LOA. [Class B divisions may be created if the number of entries warrant it.]
    Fore-and-aft vessels include: topsail schooners, schooners, ketches, yawls, cutters, and sloops.

• Class C

    All other fore-and-aft-rigged vessels with a least waterline length of 30 feet (9.14 meters)

• Division CI

    All gaff-rigged vessels of less than 100 feet (30.5

meters) not racing with spinnakers, and all vessels built before 1939 not already included in Classes A, AII, and B.

- Division CII
    All Bermuda-rigged vessels of less than 100 feet (30.5 meters) not racing with spinnakers.

- Division CIII
    All vessels of less than 100 feet (30.5 meters) racing with spinnakers.

Note - Length Overall is the length between the forward end of the sternpost and the aft end of the stem. It does not include the bowsprit, pulpit, or any other extension at the bow or stern.

Courtesy of the International Sail Training Association.

Participants in the Tall Ships® 2000 Race
Boston to Halifax to Amsterdam

Class A

KAIWO MARU
Country: Japan
Rig: barque, 4 masts
Length: 361 ft. LOA
Built: 1989, Tokyo
Tonnage: 2,879 gross
Crew: 199
Comments: Replaced 1930 *Kaiwo Maru* as Japanese
sail trainer, has identical sister ship *Nipon Maru*.

KRUZENSHTERN
Country: Russia
Rig: barque, 4 masts
Length: 375.5 ft. LOA
Mast Height: 162 ft.
Built: 1926, Wesermunde, Germany
Tonnage: 3,545 gross; 5,725 displacement
Crew: 236
Comments: Second-largest tall ship in world,
Russian war trophy converted to training vessel for
the Fisheries Ministry.

MIR
Country: Russia
Rig: full-rigged ship
Length: 358 ft. LOA
Built: 1987, Gdansk, Poland
Tonnage: 2,824 displacement
Crew: 206
Comments: Near-identical sister ship to *Dar Mlodiezy*.
Fast, two-time winner of Cutty Sark Races. Trains
marine engineers.

EUROPA
Country: Netherlands
Rig: barque, 3 masts
Length: 133 ft. LOA
Tonnage: 303 gross
Built: 1911, Hamburg
Crew: 50
Comments: Former lightship in the North Sea,
converted to sail charters in 1987.

DAR MLODZIEZY
Country: Poland
Rig: ship
Length: 357 ft. LOA
Built: 1981, Gdansk Shipyard, Poland
Crew: 194
Tonnage: 2,385 gross; 2,791 displacement
Comments: Replaced *Dar Pomorza* as Poland's
merchant navy cadet ship. Very similar to Russia's *Mir*.

POGORIA
Country: Poland
Rig: barquentine, 3 masts
Length: 154 ft. LOA
Built: 1980, Gdansk, Poland
Tonnage: 342 displacement
Crew: 51
Comments: Flagship of Polish Yacht Association, first
square-rig design of Zygmunt Choren, who designed
many new tall ships, such as *Concordia*.

CONCORDIA
Country: Canada
Rig: barquentine, 3 masts
Length: 188 ft. LOA
Tonnage: 495 gross
Built: 1992, Poland
Crew: 56
Comments: Custom-built for teaching. Designed by
Zygmunt Choren, who also designed *Pogoria*.

ROALD AMUNDSEN
Country: Germany
Rig: brig
Length: 165 ft. LOA
Built: 1952, Rorlau, Germany
Tonnage: 252 gross
Crew: 44
Comments: Built as transport for East German army in cold war, converted to sail trainer in early 1990 as employment project.

GLORIA
Country: Colombia
Rig: barque, 3 masts
Length: 249 ft. LOA
Mast Height: 130 ft.
Built: 1968, Bilbao, Spain
Tonnage: 1,300 gross; 1,097 displacement
Crew: 150
Comments: Colombian Navy sail trainer, lines based on classic German barques of 1920s and 30s.

EENDRACHT
Country: Netherlands
Rig: schooner, 3 masts
Length: 193 ft. LOA
Tonnage: 226 Thames Measurement
Built: 1974, Amsterdam
Crew: 38
Comments: Sister ship to *Sir Winston Churchill*.

Class AII

ASGARD II
Country: Ireland
Rig: brigantine
Length: 99 ft. LOA
Tonnage: 93 gross; 120 displacement
Built: 1981, Arklow, County Wicklow, Ireland
Crew: 25

Comments: Owned by Irish Navy; operated as sail trainer by the nonprofit group Coiste An Asgard

ST. LAWRENCE II
Country: Canada
Rig: brigantine
Length: 72 ft. LOA
Built: 1955, Kingston, Ontario
Tonnage: 34 gross
Crew: 24
Comments: A pioneering sail trainer; often the master is the only adult aboard.

EYE OF THE WIND
Country: United Kingdom, Canadian crew
Rig: brigantine
Length: 133 ft. LOA
Built: 1911, Schiffswerft
Tonnage: 150 Thames Measurement
Crew: 30
Comments: A trade ship converted to charter passenger work in 1973. Appeared in the movie *White Squall*.

Class B

ARUNG SAMUDERA
Country: Indonesia
Rig: schooner, 3 masts
Length: 129 ft. LOA
Built: 1991
Crew: 19
Comments: Built as a New Zealand sail-training vessel, commissioned as Indonesia's first training vessel at 1995 Arung Samudera Conference of island nations. Operated by the Indonesian Navy.

PRIDE OF BALTIMORE II
Country: USA
Rig: topsail schooner, 2 masts
Length: 170 ft. LOA
Built: 1988, Baltimore Inner Harbor
Tonnage: 185 gross
Crew: 47
Comments: Second replica built of War of 1812
Baltimore Clipper-style privateer. The first replica
sank in a squall in 1986 with four deaths.

OOSTERSCHELDE
Country: Netherlands
Rig: topsail schooner, 3 masts
Length: 167 ft.
Built: 1918, Netherlands
Tonnage: 226 gross
Crew: 34
Comments: Hauled freight across the Baltic, to the
Mediterranean, and along the African coast. Mast
removed and converted to motor coastal freighter in
1950s. Purchased for restoration in 1980, beautiful
interior woodwork.

AKOGARE
Country: Japan
Rig: topsail schooner, 3 masts
Length: 171 ft. overall
Tonnage: 362 gross
Built: 1993
Crew: 51
Comments: Goodwill ambassador for City of Osaka.
Name means "longing for the sea."

HIGHLANDER SEA
Country: USA
Rig: schooner, 2 masts
Length: 116 ft.
Tonnage: 140 gross
Built: 1924, Essex, MA
Crew: 21

Comments: Reputed to have been built to race
Bluenose, long career as Boston pilot vessel, trains
merchant cadets.

Class CI

BRILLIANT
Country: USA
Rig: schooner, 2 masts
Length: 61' 6" LOA
Built: 1932, City Island, New York
Tonnage: 30 Gross, 38 displacement
Crew: 10
Comments: Built for cruising in the 1930s, has also
been raced and used as a WW II patrol boat.
Designed by Olin Stevens, who also designed *Stella
Polare*. Owned by Mystic Seaport (CT).

JOLIE BRISE
Country: United Kingdom
Rig: sloop (gaff cutter)
Length: 72 ft. LOA
Built: 1913, Le Havre, France
Tonnage: 55 displacement, 44 Thames Measurement
Crew: 13
Comments: Originally a Le Havre pilot cutter, became
an English yacht in the 1920s, winner of countless
races, last sailing vessel to carry the Royal Mail.
Saved by a Portuguese doctor in the 1940s, bought by
Exeter Maritime Museum in 1977 for sail training.

JENS KROGH
Country: Denmark
Rig: ketch
Length: 80 ft. LOA
Built: 1899, Frederikshavn, Denmark
Tonnage: 34 gross
Crew: 25
Comments: Worked as deep-sea fishing vessel in the
North Sea until 1973.

MORNING STAR OF REVELATION
Country: United Kingdom
Rig: ketch
Length: 62 ft. LOA
Built: 1981
Tonnage: 26 gross
Crew: 14
Comments: As name implies, combines Christian fellowship with sail training.

ELEANOR MARY
Country: United Kingdom
Rig: sloop (cutter)
Length: 70 ft. LOA
Built: 1998, Petite Riviere, Nova Scotia
Tonnage: 24 gross
Comments: A "Westerman" style cutter, based on Bristol Channel Pilot Cutters of late 1800s.

Class CII

BLITZ
Country: Italy
Rig: sloop
Length: 48 ft. LOA
Built: 1998
Tonnage: 13.5 displacement
Crew: 8
Comments: Trains students for Italian sailing school and offers passenger charters.

SARIE MARAIS OF PLYMOUTH
Country: United Kingdom
Rig: sloop (Bermuda rig)
Built: 1993
Length: 39 ft. LOA
Tonnage: 14 gross
Crew: 8

MAIDEN
Country: United Kingdom
Rig: sloop (Bermuda rig)
Length: 59 ft. LOA
Built: 1980
Tonnage: 18 gross; 25 displacement
Crew: 12
Comments: With a pioneering all-female crew, won
two legs of 1989-90 Whitbread Round-the-World
Race.

CHESSIE
Country: USA
Rig: ketch
Length: 54' 1" LOA
Tonnage: 25 gross
Crew: 12
Comments:

ESPRIT
Country: Germany
Rig: schooner, 2 masts
Length: 66 ft. LOA
Built: 1995, Bremen, Germany
Tonnage: 59 gross
Crew: 16
Comments: Based on design of a wooden barge used
on the River Wessen.

ICE MAIDEN
Country: United Kingdom
Rig: sloop (cutter)
Length: 50 ft. LOA
Built: 1997, Southampton, England
Tonnage: 28 gross
Crew: 10
Comments: Named Best Newcomer in the 1997 Cutty
Sark Race.

ARETHUSA
Country: United Kingdom
Rig: ketch
Length: 72 ft. LOA
Tonnage: 43 gross
Built: 1982, Ipswich, England
Crew: 15

Class CIII

DASHER
Country: United Kingdom
Rig: sloop (cutter)
Length: 54 LOA
Mast height: 73'
Built: 1977, Gosport, England
Tonnage: 24.5 Gross
Crew: 12
Comments: Used for joint services military adventure
training. Her sister ship is *Kukri*.

HEBE III
Country: Czech Republic
Rig: sloop
Length: 40 ft. LOA
Built: 1999, Les Herbiers, France
Tonnage: 7 gross
Crew: 6
Comments: Brand-new private racing yacht.

STELLA POLARE
Country: Italy
Rig: yawl
Length: 83 ft. LOA
Built: 1965, Livorno, Italy
Crew: 18
Comments: Designed by Olin Stevens, who also
designed *Brilliant*. Sail trainer for Italian Navy.

GULLIVER OF SOUTHAMPTON
Country: United Kingdom
Rig: yawl
Length: 55 ft. LOA
Built: 1978
Tonnage: 24 gross
Crew: 8
Comments: Private yacht converted from charter
work.

KUKRI
Country: United Kingdom
Rig: sloop (cutter)
Length: 55 ft. LOA
Built: 1975, Gosport, England
Tonnage: 24 gross
Crew: 12
Comments: One of a fleet of nine Nicholson 55s built
for the British military for joint services adventure
training. Her sister ship is *Dasher*.

OCEAN SPIRIT OF MORAY
Country: United Kingdom
Rig: ketch
Length: 80 ft. LOA
Built: 1995, Ipswich, England
Tonnage: 60 goss
Crew: 25
Comments: Used for youth training by Gordonstoun
School, Scotland.

RONA II
Country: United Kingdom
Rig: ketch (Bermuda rig)
Length: 68 ft. on deck
Built: 1991, London, England
Tonnage: 40 gross; 44 displacement
Crew: 23
Comments: Gives sea experience to cadets from
urban London.

N.V. HAMBURG
Country: Germany
Rig: sloop, (Bermuda rig)
Length: 55 ft. sparred
Built: 1990, formerly *Orchidea*
Tonnage: 11.2 displacement
Crew: 9
Comments: One of the fastest boats in her class.

JOHN LAING
Country: United Kingdom
Rig: ketch
Length: 69 ft. LOA
Built: 1990
Tonnage: 54 gross
Crew: 17
Comments: Operated by Ocean Youth Trust, one of the largest youth sail-training organizations in the world.

CAPITAN MIRANDA
Country: Uruguay
Rig: schooner, 3 masts (Bermuda rig)
Length: 205 ft. LOA
Tonnage: 441 gross
Built: 1930, Spain
Crew: 86
Comments: Originally a cargo ship, converted to survey vessel for Uruguay's navy, and converted to school ship in 1978.

Courtesy of the International Sail Training Association.

Race Results
Tall Ships® 2000

Leg:	Boston to Halifax		Halifax to Amsterdam	
Position:	Overall	Class	Overall	Class
BRILLIANT	3	1	1	1
KRUZENSHTERN	2	2	2	1
MORNING STAR OF				
REVELATION	8	4	3	2
JOLIE BRISE	4	2	4	3
PRIDE OF				
BALTIMORE II	9	2	5	1
DAR MLODZIEZY	13	5	6	2
EUROPA	11	4	7	3
AKOGARE	15	4	8	2
JENS KROGH	5	3	9	4
ELEANOR MARY	14	5	10	5
OOSTERSCHELDE	10	3	11	3
EENDRACHT	Retired		12	4
MIR	7	3	13	5
EYE OF THE WIND	Retired		14	1
GLORIA	Did not race		15	6
ROALD AMUNDSEN	Retired		16	7
POGORIA	18	6	17	8
CONCORDIA	Retired		18	9
BLITZ	Retired		19	1
SARIE MARAIS				
OF PLYMOUTH	19	1	20	2
MAIDEN	20	2	21	3
ESPRIT	22	4	22	4
ARETHUSA	Retired		23	5
N.V. HAMBURG	Did not race		24	1
RONA II	29	6	25	2
GULLIVER OF				
SOUTH HAMPTON	25	3	26	3
ICE MAIDEN	28	5	27	6

Leg:	Boston to Halifax		Halifax to Amsterdam	
Position:	Overall	Class	Overall	Class
HEBE III	23	1	28	4
OCEAN SPIRIT OF MORAY	27	5	29	5
CAPITAN MIRANDA	Did not race	30	10	
KUKRI	26	4	31	6
JOHN LAING	Did not race	32	7	
STELLA POLARE	24	2	33	8
DASHER	30	7	34	9
ASGARD II	12	1	Retired	
ARUNG SAMUDERA	6	1	Retired	
KAIWO MARU	1	1	Did not race	
ST. LAWRENCE II	16	2	Did not race	
HIGHLANDER SEA	17	5	Did not race	
CHESSIE	21	3	Did not race	

A *Brilliant* Biography

When Walter Barnum commissioned a schooner from the newly formed yacht design firm of Sparkman & Stephens, he did so in no uncertain terms. His wife, Evelyn Humphrey Barnum, had inherited wealth and happily combined her resources with Walter's to make a high budget boat possible — Walter's dream boat. Barnum was a seasoned deep-water sailor, and not a man to cut corners.

In a letter to Drake H. Sparkman in 1930, after his initial meeting with the firm and before *Brilliant* had even got to the drawing-board stage, Barnum was explicit: "I believe you also understand that while the ship may never go around the world, she is to be designed as though that end were definitely in view. I feel we should always keep before us a mental picture of her hove to in the middle of the North Atlantic, with the wind at 80 miles an hour and seas in proportion."

He reminded them of an adventure survived by the *Cutty Sark* in the Roaring Forties – the great ship was swamped by seas so mountainous that, to the terrified sailors clinging to the yards aloft, her hull and deck were invisible underwater for minutes at a time. He wanted that kind of survivability built into a private yacht.

Barnum went even further. He followed up the letter with his detailed "Specifications for Schooner." He expected his new boat to be:

"1. Capable of being rolled over in a hurricane and coming up again with hull and deck opening covers intact.

2. To lie steadily in a full gale and in a heavy sea.

3. To have a rudder and steering gear as nearly unbreakable as possible including some kind of friction or spring gear at rudder head to take jars of sea when hove to — something perhaps that can be thrown in or out of gear. Suggest something similar to Electric Locomotive Driving Gear. [In fact, *Brilliant's* steering relies on a simple overbuilt worm gear connecting rudderhead to gear shaft – which has never needed

repair.]

4. To have lower masts stepped and stayed to stand any conceivable strain that might be placed upon them short only perhaps of a complete capsizing. [Estimated strain of one side of the main rigging: 78 tons.]

5. To be as heavily timbered, planked and decked as is reasonably possible, eliminating at the same time any really unnecessary weight where maximum strength or at least ample strength to meet first specification can be secured by closeness and quality of timbering, fastening, bracing, etc., etc.

6. Quality and number of fastenings to be consistent with good practice.

7. Nothing left undone to eliminate the possibility of rot anywhere.

8. Ventilation of bilges, lockers, etc., to be given full study to obtain best and most certain possible system using natural rather than mechanical circulation.

9. Every piece of material, whether wood or metal, to be literally perfect for the use intended. [*Brilliant's* builders used only nonferrous metals, for instance bronze and monel — an alloy of nickel, copper, manganese, silicon, and carbon – both highly corrosion-resistant.]"

The sturdiness of *Brilliant's* construction and the care of her workmanship are apparent. Her 1 3/4-inch teak planks over oak frames, wrote Captain Bowker in an article for *The Log of Mystic Seaport*, were "so well-shaped, fastened, and caulked, that it was not until 1978 that it became obvious that some of the seams should be recaulked." Bowker also pointed out that *Brilliant's* 1 3/8-inch bronze keel bolts did not require tightening until 1979.

Here was a yachtsman demanding literal perfection in a boat intended to be as nearly indestructible as shipwrights could make her. But lest Sparkman & Stephens balk at the prospect of building a floating tank, Barnum insisted also on performance:

"10. To be as fast and weatherly as possible, consistent with all of the above.

11. To be as handsome as possible, consistent with all of the above.

12. Hull and rig design to be in no way adversely affected by any accommodation requirements."

On the face of it, Barnum was demanding the impossible, a perfect compromise between speed and beauty on one hand, and seaworthiness and durability on the other – an exaggeration of the perennial dilemma faced by all cruising yacht builders. For *Brilliant* was indeed designed for fast cruising, not for racing, as Barnum made clear in a 1963 letter to Francis "Biff" Bowker, master of the *Brilliant* for more than 20 years: "I was most specific in planning *Brilliant* to get the idea across to her designer that she was not to be designed or built for racing. In order to nail it down, I told Olin [Stephens] flatly that I would probably never race her."

But instead of a floating tank, what brothers Rod and Olin Stephens and the Henry B. Nevins Yard of City Island, New York, produced was a masterpiece of fair lines, clean deck layout, and comfortable belowdecks, that could stand up to extraordinary conditions and, coincidentally, race with the greyhounds.

Brilliant competed in the 1932 Bermuda Race almost immediately after her April 23 launching, blew out her genoa the first night offshore, but finished close behind *Highland Light's* new course record and rated sixth on corrected time.

The following year she ran from Nantucket Lightship to Bishop Rock Light, England, in 15 days, 1 hour, and 23 minutes – a record for a vessel of her size. On that passage, she logged 215 miles a day at an average speed of over nine knots. Her near-record transatlantic passage preceded a disappointing fourth-place finish in the Fastnet Race. *Brilliant* again sailed in the Bermuda Race in 1936, finishing second.

Walter Barnum kept *Brilliant* only seven years before he sold her, for personal reasons, to General Motors attorney Henry T. Bodman. Thus did *Brilliant* become, for three years or so before going off to war, a Great Lakes cruiser out of Grosse Point, Michigan.

Emily Eaton purchased *Brilliant* in the name of her nephew, William W. Spivy, in October 1942 with the express purpose of making her available to the Coast Guard for wartime service. *Brilliant's* topsides were repainted battleship gray and at the bows was stenciled her official designation as

CGR 185. During the war, *Brilliant* operated from a base at the yacht club on St. Simon's Island, Georgia, as part of the Coast Guard Reserve's Coastal Picket Patrol. *Brilliant* and the fleet of power and sail craft pressed into service with her, many of them fine old yachts, were supposed to spot German submarines and function as a kind of early warning system against attack by sea. When the Coast Guard returned *Brilliant* to Spivey after the war, he authorized Sparkman & Stephens to find a buyer for her.

Briggs Cunningham, the sailor whose name now denotes the grommet above the tack used to downhaul the mainsail and shape its luff (the "cunningham") bought *Brilliant* at auction after the war for $9,500 with an eye to racing her. He had her repainted her original glossy white and re-rigged, at a cost of $75,000. To give her better speed in light air, he had her masts made taller by nine feet to handle bigger sails.

But postwar technology and changes in measurement rules effectively closed out the era of the racing schooner, and after *Brilliant* finished at the back of the fleet in the 1946 Bermuda Race, she rarely left Long Island Sound until her subsequent donation by Cunningham to Mystic Seaport in 1953. In the course of a colorful career, *Brilliant* had been bought four times and donated twice, finishing only a few miles up the coast from where she started, as one of only a handful of full-time sail-training vessels commissioned under the United States flag.

Cunningham, while extending her spars, had retained *Brilliant's* double gaff rig (gaff main and gaff fore). In 1958 Mystic Seaport fitted her with a jib-headed (Bermuda or Marconi) main, for greater ease in handling with teenage crews: no more need to raise a topsail, a difficult and tricky drill. This advantage is offset, some maintain (including Captain Bowker), by an increased tenderness and the necessity of reefing the main in winds greater than force five. Bowker also said that the new rig slows her down when sailing wing-and-wing; that is, running before the wind with booms on opposite sides.

Since coming to Mystic Seaport, *Brilliant* has served as a school ship, where young people learn the skills and techniques of seamanship. She has raced in local and coastal regattas, including the Classic Yacht Regatta in Newport,

Rhode Island; the Traditional Boat Weekend (now known as the Governor's Cup) of Essex, Connecticut; the Opera House Cup of Nantucket; the Mayor's Cup of New York City; and she has participated in ocean races between New England and Nova Scotia.

— Adapted from *Brilliant Passage, A Schooning Memoir*, by Philip Gerard.

Brilliant's Specifications
Length overall: 61' 6"
Waterline: 49'
Beam: 14' 8"
Draft: 8' 10"
Mainmast: 80'
Displacement: 42 tons
Tonnage: 30 gross

Wind and Sails

Beaufort Scale	
Wind Velocity in Knots (1.15 mph)	Beaufort Scale Number
None	0
1-3	1
4-6	2
7-10	3
11-16	4
17-21	5
22-27	6
28-33	7
34-40	8
41-47	9
48-55	10
56-63	11
64-71	12

Sail Selection. Schooner *Brilliant* vs. Apparent Wind

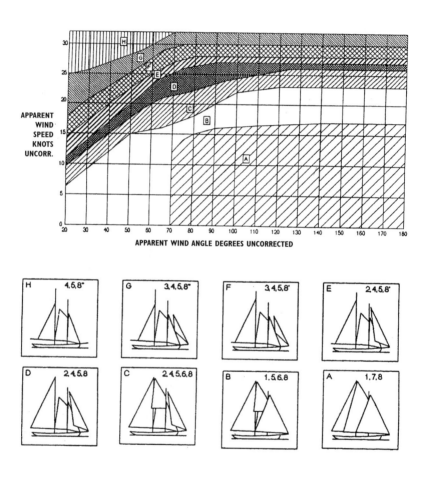

NOTE: Two sail configurations are missing here: storm trysail with forestaysail for winds above 35 knots (figure H); and for light air reaching (figure A), the number one genoa/jib would be replaced by the reacher.

Sail Chart

SAIL #	SAIL DESCRIPTION	SAIL AREA
1.	Genoa, #1 Jib	945 Ft^2
2.	#2 Jib	563
3.	Working Jib, #3 Jib	339
4.	Forestaysail	223
5.	Foresail	421
6.	Fisherman	411
7.	Golliwobbler	1,273
8.	Main	949
8R1.	Main, single reef	
8R2.	Main, double reef	

Glossary

Abaft
Aft of. The prefix a-, which is applied to many terms, means on, at, or in-the-state-of.

Abeam
At right angles to the centerline of a vessel.

Afterguard
The crew leaders on a yacht.

Beam
The measure of the greatest breadth of a vessel, or the direction at right angles to its centerline (abeam).

Beam reach
The point of sailing with the wind abeam.

Beam seas
Waves that approach the boat at right angles to its centerline.

Bear or Bearing
A term denoting the direction of an object from a vessel.

Beat
To sail to windward on successive tacks. Similarly, it means to sail with the wind as far forward as possible before the sails begin to luff (usually about 45° off the bow).

Bend
Fasten a line to something, or attach a sail to its spar.

Bobstay
A heavy stay rigged from the bowsprit tip to the stem.

Bowsprit
The spar in the stem of a vessel to which the headsails are fastened and the foremast stayed.

Broad-reach
> The point of sailing with the wind aft of abeam.

Bulkhead
> A shipboard wall or partition.

Celesticomp
> The brand name of a handheld computer used for celestial navigation.

Close-reach
> The point of sailing with the wind forward of abeam, but not as far forward as a beat.

Dead reckoning
> A procedure of navigation using course, speed, and drift data and estimates.

Field day
> A day or time set aside for cleaning up on deck and below.

Fix
> A well-established position of a ship at sea. A "running fix" is established by taking several compass bearings of one stationary object at specific intervals.

Following sea
> Waves traveling in the same direction as the boat.

Gaff
> The upper spar of a fore-and-aft, four-sided sail.

Genoa
> A large, overlapping jib.

Golliwobbler
> The nickname given to a large mainstaysail used by a schooner in light winds.

Great Circle Route
> The shortest distance between two points on the globe.

Heaving-to
> A method of securing the helm and backing some sails

while easing or lowering others to stop, slow, or steady a boat. In heavy wind and seas a vessel heaves-to in order to keep the wind forward of the beam and ride more easily to the sea.

Inmarsat
Global mobile satellite communications; also, the equipment used to access Inmarsat's services.

Jib
Generally any fore-and-aft triangular sail set on the foremast stays of sailing craft of all sizes. On a vessel with several forestays, the jib is forward of the forestaysails.

Knot
1.15 miles per hour.

Layline
The course along which a vessel can "lay" an objective (reach it without tacking).

Lifeline
Guard rails, supported by stanchions, that run from the bow of the boat to the cockpit to provide security for the crew.

LOP
Line of position (used in celestial navigation).

Luff
As a noun, the forward or leading edge of a fore-and-aft sail. As a verb, to turn a sailing craft inadvertently or intentionally into the wind and so spill the wind from her sails.

Make
Has several meanings at sea: to arrive at a desired point; to attain a certain speed; to accomplish an act, as to make (set) sail.

Mousing
A small piece of wire wrapped and twisted to secure a hook, hank, or pin.

On the nose
> When the wind comes over the bow of the boat, it is "on the nose." A sailing vessel cannot sail directly into the wind, so a wind on the nose necessitates tacking to reach a destination.

Quarter
> The section of a vessel from the beam to the stern. "On the quarter" means 45° aft of the beam.

Reef
> As a verb, to reduce the area of a sail exposed to the wind; as a noun, the portion of the sail that can be folded out of use and the result of doing so. "Double reef" refers to two such folds.

Rhumb line
> A course that crosses all meridians at the same angle. A line of constant course is a rhumb line. Over relatively short distances, a rhumb line is the shortest distance between two points.

Run
> The point of sailing before the wind. Also, the passage of a vessel from one point to another in a period of time.

Shortened-down
> Having reduced sail area; achieved by reefing or by taking a sail down altogether.

Slatting
> The slapping of sails when, lacking wind to fill them, they are tossed about by the movement of a vessel.

Spar
> A pole in the rigging of any craft, including a mast, boom, bowsprit, or yard.

Spinnaker
> A large racing sail for running or reaching.

Split tack
> Vessels being on opposite tacks.

Spreader
> Short, horizontal spars extending out from the masts that hold various stays in a desirable position or angle.

Stanchion
> Any of a number of vertical supports for rails and life-lines.

Stay
> The general term for lines of rope, wire, or bar used to support a mast. Stays are for the most part a vessel's fixed, standing rigging.

Stem
> The upright structural member forming the shape of the bow.

Taffrail log
> A log is a device that measures speed or distance traveled through the water. Historically, the taffrail is the rail around the uppermost deck in the stern of a vessel.

Take in a tuck
> To fold a portion of a sail away and out of use; to reef.

Telltale
> A pennant or streamer that shows the behavior of the wind.

Trade winds
> Relatively steady winds. In the north of the North Atlantic they are usually blowing out of the west, but in the south of the North Atlantic, especially south of 20° N, they blow out of the east.

Trysail
> A triangular fore-and-aft sail used in place of the mainsail for heavy weather sailing or as a steadying sail when hove-to.

Way
> To be in motion over the bottom. A vessel is sailed "into way" from a still position.

Wing-and-wing
    Sailing directly downwind with the headsail set to one
    side and the main to the other to prevent the main from
    blanketing the forward sails from the winds force.